W9-COH-787

The Achiever's Profile

Also by Allan Cox

Confessions of a Corporate Headhunter
Work, Love and Friendship: Reflections on Executive Lifestyle
Inside Corporate America
The Making of the Achiever

The Achiever's Profile

One Hundred Questions and Answers to Sharpen Your Executive Instincts

Allan Cox

American Management Association

This book is available at a special
discount when ordered in bulk quantities.
For information, contact Special Sales Department,
AMACOM, a division of American Management Association,
135 West 50th Street, New York, NY 10020.

Library of Congress Cataloging-in-Publication Data

Cox, Allan J.
    The achiever's profile.

    Includes index.
    1. Executive ability--Miscellanea.   I. Title.
HD38.2.C68 1988   658.4'09   88-47704
ISBN 0-8144-5796-7

©1988 AMACOM, a division of
American Management Association, New York.
All rights reserved.
Printed in the United States of America.

This publication may not be reproduced,
stored in a retrieval system,
or transmitted in whole or in part,
in any form or by any means, electronic,
mechanical, photocopying, recording, or otherwise,
without the prior written permission of AMACOM,
a division of American Management Association,
135 West 50th Street, New York, NY 10020.

Printing Number

10 9 8 7 6 5 4 3 2 1

For
Laura

What we measure we do,
What we *measure* we do,
What we measure we *do*.

Contents

An Opening Word: Skill Building

Corporations are vocal about their missions, strategies, and goals. They don't, however, content themselves by just talking about these things. They also generate reams of written material in the way of print advertising, annual reports, and internal memoranda—all spelling out what they want employees, shareholders, and the public to know about their plans and policies.

Yet missions, strategies, and goals without the *means whereby* don't take hold. They just end up being words piled upon words, with a lot of finger pointing among failed associates. What we need most is actions and attitudes that we can *measure* that help us *get* there. We must subject ourselves to specific behavior benchmarks that let us know we're on the right track and engaged in the right processes. If we don't do this, we'll never reach our goals. This book provides such behavior benchmarks, and they constitute *the achiever's profile.*

Perhaps the key concept today in conducting global business successfully is *quality*. Not just quality products and services, but corporatewide quality in every respect. Quality that is not inspection-oriented, but design-oriented; in other words, built in. This is quality that expresses itself most powerfully when people of a company become uncompromising about (1) their own unceasing growth and development, (2) designing their own improvement, and (3) ensuring that they are and remain value-added to their enterprise and to society.

Another way of thinking about *means whereby*, benchmarks, and quality is to answer a question: What quality design features are you continuing to build into your own performance profile?

Patricia Galagan, editor of *Training & Development Journal*, put forth the same notion in her inimitable way in the December 1987 issue:

> Acquired any new skills lately? I mean are you more entre-preneurial than you were this time last year? Have you mastered decision making? Just how much value have you added to your-self in the past 90 days? If you haven't acquired at least one new skill in the past six months, you probably ought to drop back a decade or two until this competitiveness thing blows over.

So the challenge to you in seeking to offer quality—to *be* quality—is *skill building*. This is not just a nice idea. It's critical. Your surviving and thriving depend on such achievement. Avoid growing, avoid the responsibility of stretching yourself, avoid being truthful about what you lack and can acquire by way of skills and enhanced strengths, and you'll find yourself on the outside looking in. *Being* quality is the way things are going. Make no mistake, this is the global drift.

Work is more demanding than ever, yet potentially more exhilarating, if we'll wake up to what it is about—namely, car-ing for that work and for the people we serve both inside and outside our corporations.

These one hundred "fast-take" chapters were written between early 1986 and early 1988. Measure yourself against the nitty-gritty, people-sensitive benchmarks they present. Then apply their lessons and you'll find that you're already sharpen-ing your executive instincts in accordance with what today's world demands. You'll assure yourself of being an achiever. This will be true whether you're engaged in high tech or low tech, manufacturing or services; whether you're an accountant, salesperson, plant employee, engineer, market researcher, CEO, or switchboard operator. It will also be true whether you're a man or a woman. In this book I have sometimes had to resort to the generic "he" to avoid awkward repeated use of "he or she." But the many examples involving women managers show that I respect them just as much as their male counterparts, and in no way mean to exclude them.

To my mind, being an achiever means you are marked by a commitment to (1) team, (2) risk, (3) balance, and (4) results.

In wending your way through this little book, you'll be asked to quiz and rate yourself on a wide range of specific actions and attitudes pertaining to these four performance areas, which are interwoven throughout. The chapter questions and answers, along with accompanying essays and action steps, provide a *means whereby* you can embark on skill building in a practical way.

Dig in. Go at your own speed. Set new standards for yourself. Most of all, have a good time and savor your achievements.

Allan Cox
Chicago, Illinois

1

A SMILE'S WINNING WAYS

Q: **Do you smile when greeting your subordinates?**

A: Usually/Often ———
Sometimes/Seldom ———

I T'S SO HARD for some people to smile. Such difficulty is born of a glum disposition about life that has been years in the making. It's clear that the austere expression of such people is a result of a tainted outlook and bad habit.

Novelists and psychologists long have taught us how the face of a human being is an X ray of his disposition and character. Our smiles convey an upbeat attitude about life, while our frowns project the opposite and cannot be explained away by gravity.

What a Frown Does

For the most part it does damage. To begin with, the frown is an intimidator and discourager. When we encounter it in a salesperson, waiter, or someone else whose job is to serve us, we begin to wonder if we've come to the wrong place. It is also a distancer. When we want to dramatize to family, friends, or work associates that we are displeased with them (justifiably or not), we often do so with our frowns. We do this rather than making a straightforward statement about what's bothering us in the offending party's actions ("I know it sounds picky, but I'd be grateful if you wouldn't smoke in my office"), or admitting that our frown is a pout to win us some attention or pampering.

This is not to say that all frowns are inappropriate. In situations where we feel grief, strong disapproval, or sudden disappointment, a frown is authentic and a smile would look out of place. But keep in mind that when such occasions arise, most people understand and sympathize with us.

What a Smile Does

For the most part, it deals out dignity. Accordingly, the answer to the question should be "usually/often." If you couldn't honestly give this answer, work at it until you can. Why? To begin with, the smile is a welcomer and a valuer. When we greet others with a smile, we take the first step toward showing their worth just by being themselves and by being *there*—in our presence. A smile is also an encourager. When we want to let a subordinate know we place importance on his ideas and performance, our smile says, "Go ahead, tell me. Go ahead, do it! I believe in you." Or even, "Yeah, you blew it on this one, Nancy, but don't take it so hard. I'm counting on you tomorrow."

One caveat: Just as frowns can be authentic, so smiles can be phony and are spotted easily. Eric Hoffer pointed out that some smiles are akin to a frightened animal baring its teeth. And one chief executive that I met recently is known (behind his back) in his company as "the smiling cobra."

Except for these instances, who wouldn't rather receive smiles than frowns? Well then, since we know this, how obvious it is for us to be spontaneous in giving them out! In fact, when it comes to smiles, be a spendthrift!

TAKE ACTION

1. Take stock. Ask three friends or family members about your smiling. Guard against touchiness if told that you act as if your face might crack. Find out whether they think your smile most often is authentic or not. If the word is good, rejoice. If not, work on your glum attitude and start practicing with your subordinates.
2. Combine your smile with firm rather than furtive eye contact. This will make your smile indicative of your real feelings in welcoming a person and will prevent the momentary smile that seems phony.

2

WHAT'S IN A HANDSHAKE?

Q: **Do you shake hands with a firm grip?**

A: Usually/Often _____
Sometimes/Seldom _____

ONE SUBJECT ON which it is easy to ascertain a meeting of minds with any large group of people has to do with the simple act of shaking hands. Almost all of us agree that being on the receiving end of a weak, limp handshake makes us feel like shuddering. This makes the better answer to the question "usually/often."

Hand-in-Hand Contact

If we turn to romance, it's clear that hand-in-hand contact is an expression of encounter, involvement, perhaps the beginnings of intimacy. Its duration over an afternoon walk in a park or an evening's *tête-à-tête* makes firmness inappropriate.

In contrast, the brevity of the handshake requires firmness in order to convey contact no less purposeful or hopeful (but just different) from romance.

Given the unanimity of positive opinion regarding the firm handshake, one wonders why many people nonetheless persist in offering the lifeless paw. For my part, I run into a fair number of executives who extend themselves this way, and, although I shouldn't be, I'm always a little surprised when they do.

Actually, such executives aren't extending themselves at all, but rather are withholding. They are saying by their behavior that firm contact with another human being is uncomfortable. Most unfortunate, such handshakes are habitual with these executives and are likely to point to a management style marked by hesitancy and a skittishness in overall team effort.

Firmness and Authenticity

While the perpetrators of weak handshakes are showing that they are moving away from you, firmness is no *guarantee* that they are moving toward you. The bone crusher is a case in point. Dominance, not encounter, is the purpose here.

Not too long ago, I had lunch with a woman who is a senior

journalist with one of the major business magazines. We had a cordial, nice enough time. She was able to pick my brains on management trends and possible story ideas, while I had the opportunity to tell her about a forthcoming book of mine. My clear hope was that she might refer to it in one of her features.

After I paid the bill (you can see who was selling!), we were about to go our separate ways. She then took my offered hand into both of hers, pumping vigorously, while gushing that not only should we stay in touch, but that I must call her anytime to get together, even on short notice.

Now there's no reason this woman *should* feel any obligation to me. My point is simply that I knew immediately from her handshake that my hope for that luncheon never would be realized. I learned long ago that the double handshake is as phony as a three-dollar bill. To test my conviction, I called her twice. She neither took my calls nor ever returned them.

TAKE ACTION

1. If you have a weak handshake, acknowledge that you are moving away from people. If your handshake is too firm, acknowledge that you are trying to dominate people, not persuade them.

2. Ask yourself: "Is this serving me well?" Then resolve to adjust your handshake style accordingly. A wise person once said, "A kiss is not only an expression of ardor; it produces it." Your handshake should not only convey your friendliness toward others, but make them feel friendly toward you.

3

THE BOSS WITH CLAY FEET

Q: **Are you unwilling to poke fun at yourself among subordinates when you make a mistake?**

A: Usually/Often _____
Sometimes/Seldom _____

IMAGINE A BOSS who laughs easily and says:

- I can't believe I went back on my word to include you in the discussion on that pricing decision.
- I can't believe I blew my stack over something so important.
- I can't believe I got upset over something so *un*important.
- I can't believe I was so hard on Sarah when it was her first attempt at writing ad copy.
- I can't believe I insisted John get an MBA when all he needed was that I provide him with a hefty challenge.
- I can't believe I said to forget about Apex, that they aren't a competitive threat.
- I can't believe I actually said this job comes before your family.
- I can't believe I tried to bluff my expertise on computers with Linda, who's forgotten more about them than I know.
- I can't believe I promoted Phil into that job.
- I can't believe I ignored the design side of that product, which guaranteed its failure with the consumer.

Such a boss knows that the answer to the question should be "sometimes/seldom."

What This Means

Bosses who are willing to admit that they have clay feet endear themselves to us. It means that warmth is characteristic of their life in general and work in particular. I define warmth as *the appetite for showing and being shown acceptance.*

You can bet that a boss who acknowledges the periodic faux pas that are inevitable for any executive—no matter how able— is a boss who is quick to forgive others for theirs. This acceptance of self and others is a bridge builder for joint initiative.

Another way to gain an appreciation for the importance

of poking fun at ourselves for our miscues is to absorb the enormous implications of this tidy little nugget of truth: If we don't acknowledge our limitations, we most certainly will doubt our strengths.

How This Shows Itself

I'm reminded of an executive vice president who is on the board of, and also the chief administrative officer of, a large, diversified food company. One day, he and the CEO concluded that the corporation needed to go outside its ranks for a top-flight human resources officer.

A search was begun, and after a few months, several outstanding candidates were identified. The candidate most preferred threw a curve at our man by saying the condition of his coming on board was to report to the CEO rather than to him, which was part of the plan when the search was undertaken.

Reluctantly, our man agreed, overcoming fears of lost turf and pique with the CEO, who'd relented on the candidate's wish. Yet, in a matter of months, he went to the new human resources officer, confided his original resentment, but then told him: "I'm so glad you're here. You've made my job easier, and this a better place." Then he told his subordinates what he'd done.

A champ.

TAKE ACTION

1. Imagine working for such a boss. Perhaps you already do, and know how fortunate you are. In that case, let your boss know how much you appreciate him in this respect.
2. Knowing how much you appreciate this in him, be sure your own subordinates can say the same about you!

4

A DIFFERENT KIND
OF THERMOSTAT

Q: **Do visitors and subordinates feel uncomfortable in your office?**

A: Usually/Often _____
Sometimes/Seldom _____

THERE ARE EVENTS that take place in all our lives that dwarf any expectations we have of them. We approach them with a sense of routine or even dread, but time and circumstance conspire in some way to convert the events into an unforgettable, perhaps life-reordering experience.

Such was the case for me when, in the early 1960s, I accepted an invitation from a friend to attend a lecture by Paul Tillich, the world-renowned theologian. "Existentialism," you may remember, was a big word on campuses and among the intelligentsia in those days, and I knew just enough about Professor Tillich to know he was a premier interpreter of it.

So I went to the lecture, with only the mild purpose of having my "current affairs" persona dusted off a bit. The lecture hall was jammed and the noise level high as the other attendees made clear by their animated conversations that they expected far more from the anticipated speaker than I did.

Over the next hour, the man himself changed all that for me. He spoke slowly, in a soft cadence of English with a German accent. He didn't smile, yet exuded warmth. He was in command of his subject and audience. He wasn't what we think of as charismatic, yet in every voice inflection, facial expression, and bodily gesture he projected powerful grace.

His presentation wasn't a sermon, but I was profoundly moved. He cared about us in the audience and wanted us to grow. So instead of this being a dry, intellectual exercise in which I added to my cocktail-party vocabulary, I was to learn that the idea feeding existentialism as a concept was *participation*. I was to have drilled home to me that existence—my life—is purposeful only when I approach it down to its minutest detail with a sense of involvement, of engagement. To this day, I repeatedly fail to comply, but I've never forgotten the marching orders of that evening.

The Minutest Detail

A minute detail in the work lives of executives is how they handle themselves when hosting visitors and subordinates in their offices. What I'm getting at here, of course, is to have you think about the degree of warmth that exists for people who have face-to-face meetings with you in your little corner of the enterprise.

You're the one in control of the emotional thermostat. You're the one who has to take the steps that allow you to answer the question "sometimes/seldom."

Your Involvement Matters

Naturally, there are times when the purpose of an office meeting is confrontation of an unpleasant issue and discomfort is inevitable. But when your involvement is extended to the visitor, even those meetings—marked as they are with strong feelings—are more likely to have beneficial outcomes than meetings where coldness, aloofness, and indifference prevail.

TAKE ACTION

1. Engaging life in its minutest details is not a soft concept; rather, it's mental toughness. Acknowledge whether you regularly devalue people by being perfunctory and distant with them while they're in your office.

2. If you find yourself doing so, point the finger of poor performance at yourself, and then acknowledge what an initiative-killer your actions are. Resolve that it is worth your time and concentration to make your office visitors feel at ease instead.

5

TEAMING UP
WITH WARMTH

Q: **Are you committed to making a team out of the people who report to you?**

A: Usually/Often _____
Sometimes/Seldom _____

LAST WEEK I spent two days with the top five marketing executives in one of the nation's major fast-food companies.

Although this company is the 600-pound gorilla in its field, it has had many organizational changes recently, including bringing in a senior vice president of marketing from the outside. All five people I met have been in their jobs less than a year, and have known their new boss for only two months.

The senior vice president quickly concluded that this group was not working well together and sought ways to improve the situation. We had never met, but he learned about me from the corporation's director of management development and asked if I could be of help. I said I thought so and agreed to meet the group.

On the first day, I met with each of the five separately to learn their responsibilities, hear their concerns, get a sense of their expectations for my visit, and let them get to know me. That evening, the senior vice president and I went to dinner. We got acquainted and I learned firsthand *his* expectations for my visit.

Warmth Inspires

We got on quickly and well. He's very bright, intense, and analytical. Nevertheless, his basic warmth came through repeatedly as he talked about his new charges, his belief in each of them, and his ambitions for them. He anticipated outstanding performance from them, and it was clear that he would celebrate their growth with them.

Whenever I work with someone, I start from where I am. By that, I mean I like to take notice of my own reactions to people and events as they unfold. As I had dinner with this new forty-year-old client of mine, I reflected on how much I liked him, admired his accomplishments up to that point, appreciated how easy he was to talk with, appreciated his commitment to his work, and appreciated his ease in asking for help as he began his new job. Most of all, I appreciated him for his commitment to make a team out of the loose, talented aggregate that reported to him.

Warmth Attracts

We agreed with almost identical wording (I had jotted down my thoughts before dinner) on two simple objectives for the next day when I'd meet with all five executives (without their boss present) at an offsite conference center. These objectives were: (1) clarify how things work between these people now and (2) clarify how things *should* work between them.

This was not a complicated task, but no more critical one existed for the marketing department. It's fair to say that the client, the five executives, and I all believe that our mission was accomplished. Some turf battles were eliminated, and five people made commitments on how they were going to team up rather than get in one another's way.

More than ever, the five feel lucky to be working with their new boss. The initiative this supportive boss has taken right off the bat has made clear that he believes in them and expects them to function as a team. Moreover, his efforts to make this the case have convinced them that they have an enviable opportunity to excel by pooling their talents and information rather than by trying to outshine one another. The positive energy that now flows in this department—converting it from a cold pantry to a warm kitchen—will make it one that younger, rising executives aspire to join.

As my client knows, the answer to the question should be "usually/often."

TAKE ACTION

1. Follow the lead of my client. Note and relish the strengths of your subordinates. Let them know that you do.
2. Demand that they find ways to act on those strengths and offer your aid in their quests. Do this and you'll discover that you have become a coveted boss and that your department has become one that up-and-comers aspire to.

6

AN IMPATIENT LISTENER MISSES THE MESSAGE

Q: **When talking with associates, do you finish their sentences?**

A: Usually/Often _____
Sometimes/Seldom _____

I HAVE FOUND that there are occasions when good can come from my finishing the sentence or sentences of someone with whom I'm discussing a subject. One of these is when I'm being told something by somebody who knows a lot more about the subject and is passing along information or views for my or our joint benefit. I can let my partner know I'm getting it and reduce his "teaching load" by anticipating where he's going and running ahead of him a little bit.

Another is when my discussion partner and I are in an animated conversation and I jump in with a connection that is an expression of enthusiasm. This constitutes a "joint eureka" and is almost always a positive experience for both parties.

These occasions are relatively rare, however, and such an intrusion normally sends out bad vibes. The answer to the question, therefore, should be "sometimes/seldom."

You Haven't Got the Words; I Haven't Got the Time

That's the message I'm sending to my discussion partner— usually unwittingly—when I finish his sentence. What I'm doing by this stealing of thunder is to set myself above by showing that I'm a quicker study and smoother tongue. It's a particularly annoying bit of self-puffery that will lead me to lose match points if I persist in it. It is a put-down of the other person that invites retaliation, though that, too, is likely to be expressed unwittingly and subtly.

The impatience shown in such interruption is also a poor use of time and a demonstration of a poor *concept* of time management. Just think how often you've finished someone's sentence only to learn that you did so incorrectly and the other person has to retrace his words to get you back on track. And even when you've been accurate in your anticipation of content, you have saved only a smidgeon of time while annoying the speaker, and you can bet that's going to cost you a lot more time later.

Message Sent; Message Rejected

Here the message I'm referring to is one being sent to *me*, but one that I reject by my guessing games and interruptions. It is the true message that should be sent but won't be because the sender has become inhibited from my having made him feel stupid or inept in the past. It's the message that is substituted with what I want to hear rather than valid information from that person who knows more about a subject or situation than I. It's the message that loses out to petty debate or outright argument when the sender vents his frustration at my know-it-all, condescending attitude. It's a message that, having been rejected, leaves both sender and intended receiver poorly served.

TAKE ACTION

1. Keep a record. If you're prone to finish associates' sentences, it's likely to be a habit far more ingrained than you're aware of. At least once a day for the next two weeks, recall a conversation you've had with someone immediately after its conclusion. Tally the frequency of your interruptions. Don't be discouraged at that number. Just be sure to repeat this exercise as often as necessary to break this habit altogether.
2. Recognize fully that the impatience shown in your rushing in to complete someone else's sentences is actually a time-waster. Providing a more relaxed environment is more fruitful. In this case, giving time is saving time.

7

MAKING AN
APOLOGY COUNT

Q: **Do you apologize to subordinates before they have fully
spoken their complaints?**

A: Usually/Often _____
Sometimes/Seldom _____

IT'S HARD TO imagine anything but good coming from an apology. After all, among all the amenities lacking in our work relations with one another, certainly an "I'm sorry—I was wrong about that" has to rank high.

Absorbing the Complaint

Yet an apology can be spoiled if it is premature. By that I mean we negate its positive effects if we offer it before we completely know what we've done that's offensive to the complaining party. This may surprise us—even annoy us—particularly when we're preparing to pat ourselves on the back for displaying our magnanimity to a subordinate!

When we stop to think about it, though, it isn't hard to discern what purpose is served by hastily admitting to an irate subordinate that we have committed some sin of omission or commission. By doing so, we divert the full force of the complaint, allowing it to deliver only a glancing blow at our self-esteem.

Obviously, then, the purpose is not a good one because it prevents us from learning from the experience. The subordinate is robbed of the chance to vent frustrations and feel heard. Moreover, in refusing to absorb the complaint, we feign genuine concern while doing nothing to solve the problem between ourselves and the subordinate. Even worse, we increase the likelihood of repeating our mistake later.

Whenever subordinates come into our office steamed up at us about something, get only halfway through their first sentence before we throw up our hands and say, "I know, I know, I'm sorry," they've just been had.

As the aggrieved, they have not been able to give full expression to what offends them. And as the offenders, we retreat without finding out how our actions may have interfered with what they were trying to accomplish for the benefit of all.

Inviting Open Discussion

To be sure, you would be right if you parried my comments by pointing out that "I know, I know, I was wrong" is actually useful. You could say that such an expression of vulnerability by the offending boss is an invitation to open discussion with the wronged subordinate.

You would be right, that is, if the *tone* in which those words were uttered implied "OK, I blew it, I know. I want you to tell me chapter and verse how I blew it, and what actions you would appreciate from me on this matter in the future." Then we could hammer out an understanding or accommodation, one that also might (but would not necessarily) include my views on how the subordinate is off base or has something yet to learn before claiming the last word on the subject.

Such an invitation is a model for all bosses who are committed to learning as well as teaching while engaged in the practice of management. What we need to guard against especially is the temptation to use an apology as a dismissal rather than being willing to listen to our subordinates fully. This makes the better answer to the question "sometimes/seldom."

TAKE ACTION

1. Acknowledge those occasions in the past year when you offered a hasty apology, not to rectify problems but to be rid of them.
2. Pledge to make your next apology a time when you're willing to absorb a coworker's complaint fully. Make it a learning event.

8

A FRIENDLY EXCHANGE

Q: Do you keep listening and speaking in fairly equal parts in discussions with another?

A: Usually/Often _____
Sometimes/Seldom _____

For SEVENTEEN YEARS I worked closely with a man who was one of the very best in his field. He's Bob Palenchar, and he retired for the second time last year. When he first stepped down from his distinguished career, he was vice president of corporate affairs for Esmark. The second time, he had served as full-time adviser to Don Kelly, the former CEO of Esmark who had then taken over Beatrice in the largest leveraged buyout in the history of U.S. business.

Palenchar's background was human resources—what we used to call personnel—and in this field he was a giant. We did numerous senior executive searches together—I as his consultant—and we traveled together extensively.

On a search, my job was to generate two or three candidates who had passed muster with me, then present them to him. He and I would travel to each candidate's city and interview the candidate together, with Palenchar taking the lead. I was there more as middleman and for taking a second look.

Palenchar was a masterful interviewer. Yet while candidates were aware of that, what most impressed them was his knowledge of his company, his grasp of its diversified businesses, and his enthusiasm for sharing that knowledge.

He best summed up his effective style one night at dinner with a candidate by saying: "The purposes of an interview are to exchange information and make a friend."

Listening

A job interview, whether the position at stake is a part-time cashier in a short-order restaurant or CEO of a company with $10 billion in sales, presents a good picture of what takes place when people come together to hold a discussion.

What takes place leads to either success or failure. I find, for example, that many of my corporate clients—the "line" executives who actually run their businesses—have to be coached not to talk too much! They're inclined to leap into the interview by describing their business, their customers, their culture, their preferences in a candidate, and their plans, problems, and opportunities.

By the time they've finished with all that, the interview time is almost up and they've learned next to nothing about the candidate and his appropriateness for the job. On the other hand, the candidate learns a lot about the job and my client— most notably that he's not a good listener.

Speaking

In contrast, there are so-called interviewers who are cold fish. They have the emotional thermostats in their offices turned down to 32 degrees and give little of themselves.

An undeniable truth in one person meeting with another is that to get worthwhile information, one must also be prepared to give it. If, for example, you have a habit of asking a lot of questions when you are together with someone, but volunteer no views of your own, your discussion partner soon catches onto your game. You may be a good listener technically, but you'll have nothing of consequence to listen to. Least of all will you have come into contact with what matters to your partner.

All these examples show that the answer to the question should be "usually/often."

TAKE ACTION

1. The exchange of information is critical. In this chapter and the next, I've used the example of the interview. It shows that in all our exchanges with people, listening counts. Realize that you give a little to get a little.
2. Watch master interviewers at work. Learn from them. Lighten up. Come alive. Make a friend. Now turn the page. You'll see that I hammer this point home even further.

9

THE DISCIPLINE OF BEING THERE

Q: **Are you an animated listener?**

A: Usually/Often _____
Sometimes/Seldom _____

Do YOU REMEMBER that absolutely hilarious movie *Being There*, which came out a few years ago? It featured the extraordinary comedic actor the late Peter Sellers in the lead role.

The character he played was a benign, inept, reclusive adult whose understanding of life and the world was limited to the perceptions he derived from television. His most revealing expression was "I like to watch." Being there, or in other words, participating in real everyday life, was not something of which he was capable.

By contrast, WTTW, Chicago's educational television station, boasts a broadcast journalist, John Callaway, who knows no peer in "being there." He is, hands down, the best on-air interviewer in the land. He has the Emmys to prove it.

Whether interviewing Rev. Ike, Ralph Nader, three women disc jockies at once, a geopolitical journalist, Tad Szulc, the CEO of a corporation, Sid Caesar, or the president of Moody Bible Institute, he makes his guest come alive for the viewer.

He does it by being an animated listener.

Discipline

The discipline employed by John Callaway serves as an example to all of us who seek to elicit meaningful information from others and pay attention to it. Let me pass along elements of that discipline that strike me as most useful. Keep in mind that the listening process involves much more than what we merely hear. It also includes what we do to open up or inhibit the flow of information.

(1) Callaway's face is elastic, his eyes alive. (2) He moves around in his chair. He gestures easily and often with his hands. He leans forward and lays back. He hunches his shoulders, then throws out his chest. (3) His voice is an instrument. It goes up and down, plays soft and loud. He speaks fast and slow, sometimes a lot, other times hardly at all. (4) His mind is always engaged. He prepares for the interview by learning everything he can about his guest, and while in session his concentration

is total. (5) He's warm and inviting, yet direct. He engenders spontaneous conversation, yet insists on what he wants to know and makes judgments without apologies. He's kind and tough. He smiles, but he also gets his Irish dander up.

Giving

Callaway's effectiveness shows that the answer to the question should be "usually/often." His performance also shows that to be a good listener—to generate worthwhile, authentic information and absorb it—we have to be authentic ourselves in the listening process. We have to give pieces of ourselves to our partner in the exchange.

Stone faces, wooden bodies, monotone voices, niggardly pronouncements, and—yes, even joking—will bring us only mirrored, echoed responses. What a waste of effort and lost opportunity for *being there!*

TAKE ACTION

1. The next time you have a conversation with someone, stop and think afterward whether you spent most of your time asking questions, making very few, if any, statements.
2. If this is the case, then ask yourself what the person learned from and about you. If little or nothing, that's what you probably learned from and about him.

10

THE MANAGERIAL DOWNSPOUT

Q: **Are you a "debater" type of listener? Do you make your conversing partners *prove* their points?**

A: Usually/Often _____
Sometimes/Seldom _____

T HERE'S A FORMER CEO of a medium-size chemicals company who's spending his retirement years in bitterness. When I was told this recently by a client of mine who used to report to him, I thought back to the one time I met him in the late 1960s.

He struck me as a pompous, blustering type—a man who reveled in being a big frog in a small pond. I arrived at his office a few minutes before our appointment, leafed through the company's house organ while sitting in the reception area, and noticed that he was prominently featured in the magazine's lead article.

Never minding that these publications are put to better use when less lordly people in the corporation are their subjects, I used the free time to learn a bit more about the man I soon would meet.

Of course, he was described in almost messianic terms and praised for his management style. That style was marked, said the writer, by keen incisiveness, a gruff exterior, and bluntness. I learned from that piece that one of his opening gambits when a subordinate came to him with a proposal was, "Are you ready for a *grilling* on this?"

Grilling, Not Exploring

Now, nobody believes any more than I do that a potentially good idea can't come of age unless it's discussed. Moreover, if such discussion is to work, it has to be intense. But the intensity is one of joint involvement and emotional investment of all the parties to the discussion.

My quarrel, then, with this CEO is not that he said he wanted to get beneath surface matters and political niceties, but that he took such glee in conducting the grilling! As a result, he seldom heard his managers' best ideas. The communication was all one-way, with him as judge, and he served as a stormy managerial downspout. He enjoyed the fact that his executives approached him in a state of terror.

The man was not a listener but a pronouncer. One of the intriguing ironies of a sophisticated division of labor, which is characteristic of the modern corporation, is that subordinates know more about the technology of their business than their boss does. Commonly, subordinates are able to gang up and "fire" their boss. In other words, they give him plenty of rope to hang himself. They do so by shutting him off—or allowing him to shut himself off—from critical information.

The Debater

The debater is someone who must be right. The debater is picky, picky, picky. The debater wants to be smart while showing that you're dumb. The debater has open mouth and closed ears. The debater doesn't receive information, doesn't explore alternatives as a collaborator, but instead plays the Oracle at Delphi.

The answer to the question should be "sometimes/seldom." This CEO never knew that. And when his company failed to grow from lack of initiative, and was taken over by a conglomerate, he was shocked. Now he grieves, but nobody grieves for him.

TAKE ACTION

1. Learn from your subordinates. They know more about a lot of things than you do.
2. Say often: "Tell me about this. I don't understand."

11

SEEKING
THE MASTER

Q: Do you seek a mentor who
will test your abilities to their
fullest?

A: Usually/Often _____
Sometimes/Seldom _____

"**S**EEK" IS AN action verb. The seeker is on alert—scanning, then probing; listening, then replaying what he hears; sensing; feeling; tracking, then locking in. Seekers aim to find, and although they won't always succeed, their quest assures enlarged perspectives and more options.

Hunger for Growth

Achievers are eager to learn and seek to be taught by masters of their crafts. As you would expect, then, the answer to the question should be "usually/often."

Nonetheless, what's difficult for you, if you're like most of us, is that although you want to be known for mastery of key tasks and specialized knowledge, such competence comes at a high price. That price is working for a boss who believes in your innate hunger for growth and will accept nothing less than your best.

The difficulty is compounded, too, by the fact that not only will criticism, demands, and stress come your way from this master, but *you* have to take the initiative to find that person—whether in your company or a new one—and convince him that you're a promising learner.

As you prove yourself a person of caring and skill, your company naturally will have its own ideas for your job placement. But there always will be occasions when, for the sake of your development, you must search and campaign for placement with that teacher who will now and then make your life miserable.

Testing Your Limits

I believe it's obvious, but let me emphasize that my message here is positive. The boss I have in mind who now and then makes your life miserable is not doing so for sadistic pleasure. Nor will you, in seeking him out, do so for masochistic need.

Rather, the two of you enter a training "contract" in which the terms are designed to call upon your full capacities for achievement.

Like all good contracts, this one works to the benefit of both parties. Yes, you are given grief when you are sloppy in your work and overly fearful of taking risks with your talent. Yes, your boss has pangs at working you so hard, and wonders at times whether you're going to make it. But at the apprenticeship's end, when you begin to "get your legs," your exhilaration builds as you experience how much you can actually do. And your boss shares that exhilaration for having been the agent of your blossoming.

TAKE ACTION

1. Be alert to your strengths that need nurturing at the hands of a master. Name three or four higher-level managers in your company who might have the concern and ability to bring you along in these areas. Then find ways to get to know them better to confirm your suspicions. Never mind the hesitancy in your innards; choose the one most appropriate to your needs at this point. Lay the groundwork to convince your new master and all concerned that this is a good idea.
2. Someday, if not today, you will play master. Go back and thank the people who taught you how. This is one more mutual benefit to the contract.

12

GOOD BOSSES,
BAD BOSSES

Q: **Do you avoid working for
bosses who push you, stretch
you?**

A: Usually/Often _____
Sometimes/Seldom _____

IN CHAPTER 11, I wrote that it is a good thing for executives to seek bosses who push them to their limits. There's nothing about that chapter I want to retract, but will admit that it's a lot to ask. To expect people to try to be put to the test rigorously is unrealistic.

Running From Exposure

Let's assume for the moment that your personal life is in some sort of delicate balance, and the last thing you need right now is a job that will consume your mind and energies for the next year.

Or let's understand you've just come off a two-year crash program where you worked for a boss who gave you a whole new consciousness of what the "learning curve" means. You're exhilarated, but exhausted mentally and physically. Spent.

If your current state of affairs is anything like these, you can be excused from seeking a boss who'll tax you. Or you can be given the green light to sidestep involvements likely to put you under the thumb of one.

My concern, therefore, isn't for anyone in these situations, but for people who arrange their entire work lives so that they avoid ever being put to the test. They make themselves victims of low expectations.

Not only do they refuse to seek opportunities and volunteer initiative, but whenever situations arise where they fear they may be asked to join some effort by a demanding boss who has shown interest in them, they go to great lengths to render themselves invisible.

It's not surprising, then, that I consider the better answer to the question "sometimes/seldom."

The Bad Boss

Related to being put to the test in a good way is being put to the test in a bad way. My earlier comments were about seeking exposure—or at least not avoiding it—to bosses who, despite occasional abrasiveness, have your development in mind when they call upon your full capacities. Here my advice is about what to do when subjected to the bad apple.

Some people are able or fortunate enough to move through a lifelong career without having to undergo working for one. Most executives, however, have to get past such an experience, and the wise ones do everything they can to make sure that the experience doesn't damage them.

By bad apple I mean *bad*. I'm talking about the liar, cheat, backstabber—the certified scoundrel. These are the bosses who, no matter how cloyingly they may present themselves—if indeed they're trying to keep their motives under wraps—are out for their own gain at your expense.

However, believe it or not, this situation can work to your benefit if you will grit your teeth and follow one main rule: as long as what you do is not illegal or unethical, do everything you can to make your boss look good while you work for him.

TAKE ACTION

1. The next time a demanding boss asks for your contribution, swallow your timidity and give it.
2. Support the bad boss if you get stuck with one. In doing so, you're more likely to disarm him, win the admiration of higher-level managers (who aren't blind to his character defects), raise your self-esteem by coping, and emerge stronger than ever!

13

AN UNAPOLOGETIC OFFERING

Q: Do you believe yourself capable of adding a worthwhile dimension to an associate's life?

A: Usually/Often _____
Sometimes/Seldom _____

$\mathbf{M}$Y HOMETOWN HAD ten elementary schools. Each school had a Cub Scout pack, and each pack a slow-pitch, 12-inch softball team. These ten teams made up a summer league. At the season's end, the league champion played a final game against an all-star team comprising the best players from the other nine teams.

On the first Saturday after school was out, one summer almost four decades ago, I found myself the starting left fielder in a place called Ridgeland Commons for Longfellow School's Cub Pack 23.

This was my first experience in organized sports, and I was there because Mr. Jacklin put me there. Phil Jacklin was my best friend's dad, our cubmaster, and the driving force behind the summer league. He wasn't merely a well-intentioned father doing his best, but a superb athlete who knew the game, taught us how to play it, and was magnificent with kids.

Twelve weeks later, under the lights at a commercial stadium (a big deal for a bunch of twelve-year olds!), I was the starting left fielder for champion Pack 23 in the all-star game. We won 12 to 0.

Later, Phil Jacklin took me aside to teach me the rudiments of being quarterback for our eighth-grade football team. We were good because Jimmy Tregay was a fabulous halfback, but at least I got to call the plays, throw a few wobbly passes, and do the punting.

A Healthful Presumption

When an adult steps into someone's life in the formative years, we see this as a desirable, natural process. The impact of Phil Jacklin on my life—of which sports was only one part—I can attest was enormously positive, and I'm sure you have no reason to doubt me.

On the other hand, as adults ourselves, we most often consider it a presumption to step into the lives of our associates. We're willing to consider this with a subordinate, but get cold feet contemplating it with a peer, and find the process with a higher-level manager unthinkable.

It won't be surprising to you that I occasionally lose business I'd really like to have. Sometimes my sales pitch lacks inspiration, or there's simply a lack of chemistry between myself and a client. But in this chapter I'd like to tell you about a piece of business I won. I met with two principals of a giant company that I had never worked for. They were comparing my services in executive search with those of a few other firms. I wasn't told directly, but you'd have a hard time convincing me that the reason my services were sought over my competitors' is that I was willing to be a bit presumptuous.

A Worthwhile Dimension

My presumption in this case was that I stated brazenly to my prospects that headhunters are a dime a dozen (there are 1,500 firms in almost 2,500 locations listed in *The Directory of Executive Recruiters*) and that I had better be able to bring more to a party than a dutiful digging up of individuals who meet predrawn specifications. "Otherwise," I told them, "how could I distinguish myself from the pack?"   Actually, such spadework is the easiest part of search work. The "value-added" factor is judgment about candidates and the structure into which they're expected to fit. Or even judgment about whether a search should be undertaken. Or sometimes my search-evaluation study reveals that the decision-making style of the chief executive assures the failure of any candidate, no matter how good.

In this case, the "value-added" required was that the headhunter be someone not overly impressed or cowed by senior executives; someone willing to probe without hesitation into the backgrounds, attitudes, successes, and failures of the likely candidates for the position; and someone willing to demonstrate this with the senior executives in the prospective client company who are charged with considering the use of his services.

Before being awarded the search, I was told by my prospects, who had by now met with all search firms contending for the assignment, that my per diem fee was "way above the rest—not even close." I stood my ground.

A day later, I was asked to get to work. I responded, completed the search, and am pleased to report that the vice president I brought in is performing in an exemplary way. Moreover, this company has come back to me for repeat business. I believed these clients needed my services, that they would benefit from them more than they would from those of my competitors, and I said so.

One may indeed be foolishly presumptuous, which is always a risk when we're bold. But to seldom give to other people what they can use yet don't know how to value is irresponsible. This makes the preferable answer "usually/often."

TAKE ACTION

1. Start this giving process by naming one person at work who needs what you've got.
2. Come on now, don't get cold feet. Find a way to give it. You'll be surprised at how much this effort is appreciated.

14

ON BEING A TREE

Q: **Do you avoid intervening in an associate's life?**

A: Usually/Often _____
Sometimes/Seldom _____

I CONDUCT A small-group strengths development workshop for corporate officers. It's intense, lasts four days, and is limited to eight top executives from eight companies. One executive per company is desirable because self-disclosure is required of participants.

The workshop strikes executives as weird when they hear about it. Its theoretical base combines the psychologies of Alfred Adler and Frederick Perls. Participants provide me with half a dozen early recollections in advance of the session (Adler), and during the session are called upon to role-play *nonhuman* roles (Perls).

After breaking with Freud, Adler developed the early recollection technique as a means of assessing a client's style of life. He believed that by remembering what we remember and *how* we remember it, we reveal how we look at life today.

Perls, a pioneer of Gestalt psychotherapy, developed a technique—first demonstrated by genius psychodramatist Jacob Moreno—where his client sat in a chair, with an empty chair before him, and conversed with an imaginary person or thing in the empty chair.

In my workshop, I insist that the other chair be occupied by a "thing," selected by the participant from one of his early recollections.

The Thing

An early recollection is a one-time event occurring in the first six or eight years of a person's life.

The following is *not* an early recollection: "Every day on my way to kindergarten, I stopped to say hello to Mr. King. He ran a corner grocery store in our neighborhood and I liked him very much." But this is: "When I was about age seven, I took my father's ax out of the garage and went out to chop down a tree in the woods behind our house. I did it, and shouted 'timber,' then ran in the direction the tree was falling. It just missed me by inches. I was lucky, but felt stupid."

In the workshop, in the presence of all, I would have the executive play one or more objects from the recollection. Examples are the woods, ax, tree, house, or garage. Having six recollections to choose from, each executive has an almost limitless supply.

The Purpose

The recollection is the executive's own creation. Everything in it is his composition and has meaning for him whether he recognizes it or not. Since there's no script for the role, and since there are no set rules for how woods or a tree or a garage will act, he's on his own, and we get an unembellished rendition of what kind of tree, say, he is. He can't fake it as he could a human role.

My task in this workshop is intervention, and in this setting that means to get all participants involved in each role-playing segment, with one purpose in mind: to have the character at center stage get a handle on aspects of himself that he's been ignoring. I want him to *feel* those aspects, to own them by acting them out.

My intervention helps people who may at first be baffled by the process. They may think they need this like they need a hole in the head, and feel silly going through the exercise.

Yet it's a powerful medium. When an executive pretends to be a tree, and in the process of winging it begins to swagger and then introduce into the story some inept underling putting an ax to his lower trunk, he may become aware that he's been lording it over people lately and is asking somebody to topple him.

At first I was fearful about using this process, uneasy about intervening with top executives. But I soon was to learn that my risks in eventually putting it to work would be rewarded. John Lux, the dynamic CEO of Ametek—a *Fortune* 500 high-tech equipment manufacturer—attended one of these sessions and wrote me the following: "If I had missed this seminar there are a lot of things in my life and my associations that I would never have understood. The benefits will go on for years."

Many types of intervention can be very effective. This is why the answer to the question should be "sometimes/seldom."

TAKE ACTION

1. Perhaps you're avoiding an intervention with someone who would benefit a great deal from it. Steel up and stop underrating yourself.
2. You have an idea or skill. Don't be fearful to admit it. You know it's good. Put it to work with someone.

15

ENCOURAGING AUTHENTICITY

Q: **Do you enjoy helping make an associate courageous?**

A: Usually/Often _____
Sometimes/Seldom _____

SOME WEEKS AGO, I attended a national conference on business ethics where one of the principal speakers was John Filer, the imposing, retired CEO of Aetna Life & Casualty Company of Hartford, Connecticut. His entire presentation was absolutely first-rate, but he riveted my attention at one point when he described a corporatewide project he launched that required the maximum effort of each member of the company's management team.

Filer signed off on a slogan for the project that captured the sense of commitment required to make it fly. Here's how it went: "If you are what you do, when you don't, then you aren't."

Then, last night I attended a lecture by gnomelike Joseph Chilton Pearce. Pearce is an author who caught my attention in the early 1970s with a magnificent, well-researched little book entitled *The Crack in the Cosmic Egg*. This is a book that documents our formidable but unused creative powers.

Just like Filer, Pearce dropped a line on the audience that I found memorable. Here's how it went: "The heart is another form of intelligence." Pearce meant this literally, not figuratively. He said that what the mystics knew centuries ago is just now beginning to be recognized by medical science. Then he cited Dr. Christiaan Barnard, first heart transplant surgeon, who has said recently that we must discard the artificial heart. We must do so because we have learned that the heart is much more than a pump.

Finding the Heart

Whether Pearce and Barnard are correct in their literalness is certainly beyond my competence. Yet what isn't beyond my understanding is that we all have to dig for a deeper source than our brains for calling up our courage.

Someone has said, "Fear has many eyes, courage only one." And William James, the great psychologist and philosopher, said, "Emotions are not always subject to reason, but they are always subject to action."

I have my own statement to audiences of executives when I'm speaking to them on the necessity of moving out of their comfort zones, and when their likely reaction is that I'm asking them to be what they're not. The statement comes in the form of a question: "Have you ever thought that what you consider an act is really you, and what you consider you is really an act?"

Finding the Soul

When I survey my twenty-three years as a management consultant, the executives who strike me as most effective are not those who always did things right or had the ideal style. Instead, they are those who are *authentic*. Not what they *wish* they were, or *tell themselves* they are, but what they *really* are.

They realize that their authenticity and that of their associates are what generate superior, exhilarating performance. Yet being what we really are takes courage. Getting what's inside out and expressed is risky. To encourage another is not mere mild support. It is *to make courageous*. Helping our associates take heart in expressing their own authenticity makes us executives with soul.

This is the reason why the answer to the question should be "usually/often."

TAKE ACTION

1. Pay careful attention to all your associates whom you believe in. See the facets of them that they don't believe in yet.
2. Tell each of them what you see, however you think best. Then celebrate with them every move they make toward that authenticity.

16

IS
POSITIVE THINKING
A SHAM?

Q: **Do you reject the notion that thinking positively is an attitude you can cultivate in yourself?**

A: Usually/Often _____
Sometimes/Seldom _____

No matter how well conceived, the words "positive thinking" make me uneasy. I'm not alone. In routine conversation and casual reading, I've learned that the term often generates mild derision to outright repulsion from others. This is hardly puzzling. Many have the sense that the term usually gets trotted out by manipulative—or at best simplistically thinking—people in support of tawdry or hopeless causes.

The Affirmative Emotions

Yet if unease is a decoy to our missing the critical reservoir of initiative and strength residing in the concept's affirmation, we do ourselves an injustice. We throw out the baby with the bathwater.

It was Norman Cousins who brought this idea home to me most poignantly. In his moving book, *Anatomy of an Illness*, he tells how he overcame an irreversible, crippling disease by what he called "a systematic and full exercise of the affirmative emotions." Now, Cousins is not a simplistic thinker. Moreover, this man, who has written several books and was for over three decades editor of *The Saturday Review*, was known as a demanding boss.

His heroic victory can't be described fully in this space, but his self-determined treatment, at which his doctor swallowed hard, then approved, started with Cousins viewing old episodes of *Candid Camera* to make himself laugh. He reasoned that since it was known that depression and apathy are multipliers of disease, why wouldn't their opposite emotions fight it? He was rewarded for his belief as he literally began to laugh his way back to health. His experience teaches that the answer to the question should be "sometimes/seldom."

Workable, Beneficial Options

Cousins's actions also teach a lesson on options. Dispensing with all the froth, here's my definition of positive thinking: *The life-style-wide mental capacity to seek and find workable, benefi-cial options.* This definition takes the idea out of the realm of Pollyanna and places it squarely within our ability to create opportunity. It doesn't imply that we support hopeless causes, but instead urges discipline in rejecting defeat as the first and only option on some problem or tough project.

Nor does this definition demand that we ignore discour-agement when it comes our way. On the contrary, discourage-ment sometimes serves as a useful signal that another tactic might work better—other than our just giving up. In any event, we needn't be saddled with discouragement for long, whether we help it along or it passes of its own accord. And when it passes we're left ready to get on with our chores resourcefully. Executives who get results have options. Executives who have options get results.

Finally, let me stress this definition clarifies that option finding, at its best, extends to all three of our life tasks: work, love, and friendship. Sometimes my work is dull. This may be because I devote myself to it to the exclusion of my family and community. My work is dull because I'm dull, because I face my job with the imagination of one-third of a person.

Whenever you discover a workable, beneficial option and act on it, you encourage yourself to keep it up. As you do, you cultivate the attitude of thinking positively.

TAKE ACTION

1. Jot down one main challenge you face at work, at home, and with your friends or community. Acknowledge which of these, if any, you face with negative emotion. Recognize that this is likely to multiply your failure.
2. Along with your work, be sure to embark on a search for workable, beneficial options for the challenges you face at home and with your friends or community.

17

A TALE OF
TWO DREAMERS

Q: **Do you find yourself engaged
in hopeless causes?**

A: Usually/Often _____
Sometimes/Seldom _____

ABOUT HALF MY consulting practice involves executive searches. This means I'm retained to deliver to corporations the best top executives I can find.

In my book *Confessions of a Corporate Headhunter*, published over a decade ago, I said that many executives I recruit whom I deem best for a situation aren't people with whom I necessarily would want to spend a Saturday night.

Let me add quickly that this would be no great loss to them! On the other hand, I'll describe two executives I relish spending personal time with, but never would recommend to a corporate client. This is because even though in current parlance they could be called positive thinkers, they habitually become mired in hopeless causes. This is the tip-off that the answer to the question should be "sometimes/seldom."

Hopeless by Perception

The first executive graduated from the Harvard Business School. His undergraduate work was in engineering, and he's bright as a strobe light. On top of it, he's articulate, oozes with charm, and radiates charisma. In earlier days, higher-level executives cocked their heads to listen to him, while junior executives rallied round, ready to follow wherever he led.

He has management ability, too. By that I mean he is personally organized and knows how to delegate authority and responsibility. His people operate with a free hand. The spirit in any group he directs runs high—at least at the beginning of a project.

Things inevitably come apart, however, because this man is perpetually the dreamer. His execution is good, but his "galvanizing idea" is lousy, unworkable, totally impractical. Yet he's so persuasive and enthusiastic that he was able to crank himself up and get others to go along.

"What a creative guy," they said of Larry many years and several employers ago. Then most recently from a company president who thoroughly likes but fired him: "I just knew that anything Larry was a part of was going to come crashing down."

Hopeless by Performance

The second executive works in the not-for-profit arena. I met him while engaged in community activities. He, too, is well educated, having earned a graduate degree in literature from Princeton. And he, too, is articulate and charismatic; he can charm the birds right out of the trees. He's at ease in the executive suite; I've sat and watched while he adroitly won funding for his projects from corporate chieftains.

He was able to do so because, unlike Larry, his "galvanizing ideas" were good, even brilliant; brilliant because they had been overlooked, but their time for implementation had come.

Yet he was a dreamer on performance. He could think it, sell it, but not do it. He routinely thought things would work themselves out, though his agency was in disarray from his personal disorganization and unwillingness to set and stick with priorities. His funding dried up and the agency folded. "A victim of the recession," he said. Then he moved to another city and repeated his failure.

TAKE ACTION

1. Unlike these men, avoid hopeless causes and causing hopelessness. Dream dreams. But see them for the kernel of an idea that *might* work if tailored to reality.
2. Acknowledge that dreams are needed, but it's the quality of execution that determines whether they come true.

18

THREE LITTLE WORDS

Q: **Do you choose involvements where you have a distinctive contribution to make?**

A: Usually/Often _____
Sometimes/Seldom _____

I HAVE AN uncle living in Atlanta who recently sent me a cartoon from *The New Yorker* that he'd clipped sometime in the early 1970s. For a couple of decades, he was in charge of acquisitions for the Georgia State University library, so I shouldn't have been surprised that this literate, observant cataloguer par excellence would be able to dip into the past to come up with just the right device to make a point with me.

The cartoon's setting is a cocktail party taking place outdoors on a large patio. In the background, the party's jam-packed with the usual small-talkers. The foreground, however, focuses on three people: a married couple seated stiffly on a love seat, drinks in hand, passively listening to a man perched on the end of a chaise lounge. He's leaning forward, apparently earnest in what he says: "I used to be a management consultant, but now I'm into making up songs and poems."

My uncle sent this cartoon to me, I gather, because he noted a long piece of doggerel I wrote in my recent book *Inside Corporate America*, and wanted to make sure I wasn't banking on making a living this new way. "Stick to your knitting," he seemed to be saying.

He needn't have worried. Had I been so tempted (which I wasn't), I would have been cured of it in 1974 when I published another book in which I included a couple of poems I'd written. One reviewer, CEO of a major advertising agency, said my poetry made Rod McKuen read like W. H. Auden!

Lack of Conviction

While my uncle's good-natured concern wasn't necessary in this particular case, the lesson of his message is a good one to keep in mind for other occasions. Those are the ones when, as is common, we allow ourselves to get caught up in some activity where our gifts are lacking and sense of conviction is, at best, lukewarm.

The faces and postures of the two listeners in the cartoon say it all. Both are marked by embarrassed smiles and rigid carriage. What they are hearing is not absurd in its own right, but the speaker, from whom they are in retreat, is totally out of his league. His words, despite his attempt at sincerity, carry no conviction.

Perhaps our involvements aren't out-and-out laughable, but we fail to convince in many of our endeavors because we simply don't belong there. Our choices show that we aren't able to give the preferable answer, "usually/often," to the question.

Telltale Words

Three defeatist words in our vocabulary are "should," "ought," and "try." Whenever I hear someone (or myself) using these words in connection with an undertaking, I know that nine times out of ten, it won't come to fruition. Should, ought, and try are statements of good intentions, and my experience is that spoken good intentions usually are substitutes for performance.

On the other hand, when we have chosen involvements where we have our best to give, those three words rarely are used.

TAKE ACTION

1. Review all major projects you're a part of. Examine your sense of conviction about each one.
2. For those where your disposition employs the words "should," "ought," and "try," ask if it would be more constructive for you to place your efforts elsewhere.

19

WORK AS A CALLING

Q: **Do you relate your work to some higher purpose, to seeing how it improves the lot of mankind?**

A: Usually/Often _____
Sometimes/Seldom _____

LAST SUNDAY I was in church and heard a peach of a sermon. The church was Chicago's historic Fourth Presbyterian, and the preacher was Dr. John Buchanan. The sermon hit home with me because it dealt directly with what I was pondering for this chapter.

Its title was "Stepping Back from Life," and it drew from two texts. The first was from Exodus, where Moses ascends Mount Sinai for forty days and receives the laws to govern Israel. The second was from Matthew, where Jesus goes into the wilderness for forty days in preparation for his mission.

Some readers will remember that in the latter story, Jesus was tempted in the wilderness by Satan three times. After Jesus prevailed, the text says, "Then the devil left him, and behold, angels came and ministered to him."

After some discourse about the value of selective retreat and withdrawal, Dr. Buchanan concluded his sermon with these words: "May I propose that we not fail to be where the angels can find us?"

Being Found

Being found by the angels means to avail ourselves of the good news. And the good news on the job is that work has high purpose. Remember, though, that such purpose is not merely the province of the pious. It belongs to all of us who take time to think about what our labors do for people. Or what they can be made to do.

Let me be ridiculously obvious for a moment. Consider the purpose of a freeway. Think of travelers on vacation; commuters getting to work; a parent returning home to children after a long day; ambulances, fire trucks, and police cars rushing to their destinations.

Now think of a carpenter's laborer. In the case of a freeway, this might have been the person who hauled nails, lumber, or tools to the craftsman building forms according to a blueprint from a civil engineer. These forms held concrete poured from cement-mixing trucks. When the concrete hardened, the beginning of a sewer system was in place. All this was 60 feet below ground, making sure that when the rains came, drainage would be sure and the road passable. This example illustrates that the answer to the question should be "usually/often."

The Divinity of the Mundane

What I'm talking about, of course, is the divinity of the mundane and work as a calling. Robert Pirsig wrote *Zen and the Art of Motorcycle Maintenance*, the enormously popular book among young people in the 1970s. One of his points is that subjects of the day-long contemplations of Zen masters are tame compared to the goings-on in an eight-hour shift on an assembly line. Imagine if we could combine just a touch of the master's introspection with our efforts on our job, whatever it is. What a difference that would make!

We need to step back from all of the busyness to see what we're about that's wonderful. And where we discover that we're missing the point, we can make changes. One of the ironies I frequently have had to face (when will I learn?) is that a time-pressured existence is anything but a clear indication of a full life. On the contrary, when such overcrowding has occurred, I've usually found that it sneaks up on me. Then it is only by looking back over the past few days or weeks that I discover that my burst of activity has served to divert me from some embarrassing simple act or thought at work that would bind me closer to my associates and thereby put me in touch with the angels.

TAKE ACTION

1. Make your job more meaningful by thinking through all who benefit from your quality performance, then who at work is depending on you to get the job done right. Realize how important you are.
2. Before going to bed tonight, be thankful for the gift of work. Realize how fortunate you are.

20

FINDING YOUR FOLLOWERS

Q: **Do you dread having to play the persuader's role?**

A: Usually/Often _____
    Sometimes/Seldom _____

IT'S AMAZING, ISN'T it, how some seemingly insignificant events stay with us for life? For example, I've had recurring thoughts of an American history course I took when I was a sophomore in high school. It was taught by a woman named Blanche Oxborrow, and she was, without question, the finest classroom teacher I ever had.

I didn't like history, but she turned me around. She made Henry Clay and Stephen Douglas and Alexander Hamilton come *alive*. From her—not our textbook—my fellow students and I even learned about Dr. Mudd, the physician who treated the injured John Wilkes Booth after he shot Lincoln. Now you know, if you didn't, where the expression "Your name will be mud" comes from.

One day in her class, she staged a debate. The two opponents had been given their assignments in advance and were prepared. The rules were the usual: opening statements, rebuttals, closing statements.

I can't recall the subject of the debate, but I remember Don Rogers. He was one of the debaters. I didn't know him, never was introduced to him, and never saw him again after he graduated from high school that year.

He sticks in my mind, and the memory of that event periodically wedges its way into the foreground of my thought because I was so dazzled by the strength of his argument and presentation. His poise and command were remarkable in a seventeen-year-old.

A Lesson From Memory

I believe we retain particular events from our past to underscore some lesson we think needs learning or reinforcing. I certainly hold that's true for me in this case of remembering a confident young boy before a class of thirty peers in 1953. The lesson of 1953 still applies now.

Moreover, I believe we sift, sort, and select activities that drill the importance of that lesson into our minds. Continuing my example, I make every effort to catch *The MacNeil/Lehrer NewsHour* on TV, and my favorite general news periodical is *U.S. News & World Report*.

Both this broadcast and magazine, more than their competitors, work hard at having featured people on camera and page present their own points of view. The viewers and readers are then left to draw their own conclusions about what they've seen, heard, or read.

Winning Support

The lesson I think worth learning and having reinforced has nothing specifically to do with objectivity or equal time. Rather, it has to do with *belief* and speaking or writing strongly on its behalf to win support for it. Nor is the lesson about our playing the reader's or listener's role. Rather, it is to learn to be the *persuader*. People who have learned how to do this know that the answer to the question should be "sometimes/seldom."

Drs. Michael Lombardo and Morgan McCall of the Center for Creative Leadership have conducted numerous fascinating studies of executive behavior and attitude. Among their findings is that what executives dread most in their tasks is making a presentation.

John Connellan, CEO of The Executive Technique, a company that helps executives develop their presentation skills, tells me, "We really don't like ourselves very much." I agree with him and think if we can learn what young Don Rogers knew, we'll all like ourselves a lot more.

TAKE ACTION

1. Appreciate that having your views known to opponents also makes them apparent to potential supporters.
2. *Speak up* to find people who value what you give and give what you value.

21

THE CORPORATE JUNGLE: AN OVERWORKED IMAGE

Q: **Do you believe that executives in a corporation cooperate with one another more than they compete?**

A: Usually/Often _____
   Sometimes/Seldom _____

PURVEYORS OF THE corporate-jungle and rat-race outlooks argue that corporate life is dominated by character assassination, back-biting, or any brand of political infighting you can name.

Nobody is naïve enough to believe that these negative experiences in human affairs don't exist. In fact, they have a share of each day's activities in the executive suite. But they are overwhelmingly subordinated to the quantity of cooperative enterprise among executives. For this reason, the answer to the question should be "usually/often."

Enveloped by Cooperation

Competition catches our eye precisely because of its minority status. That, and because it sometimes makes a better story. Cooperation is to us like the water in which fish swim. I remember seeing a cartoon from *The New Yorker* once that showed two fish walking ashore, with one saying to the other, "This is where the action is." Their attention, distracted by dry land, would soon and hurriedly be directed back to the environment that sustains them.

Even in war—the ultimate competition—there are international rules of conduct, which combatants adhere to for the most part. When we think of our relations with the Soviet Union, we're struck by how our uneasy balance with that nation is maintained through a well-defined system of protocol. And in sports, we can't help but be aware that the game itself can go forward only by the competitors abiding by a wide assortment of ground rules. A game of any kind is at miminum 90 percent cooperation.

The "game" in the executive suite is no different. Moreover, it hardly needs to be argued that the bulk of competition there is beneficial. Most of us know that whether the competition is between peers, departments, or companies, better performance is encouraged. Without competition, many of us get a little lazy, sloppy, or downright arrogant. Don't we all consider monopoly a bad thing?

Competition Run Amok

The problem is cheating, or what I call competition run amok. This, rather than legitimate competition, is what fascinates the purveyors of the corporate-jungle and rat-race outlooks. Yet while the actions they describe are much less frequent than they would have us believe, what is important is that such actions do occur. Furthermore, they may have been characteristic of all of us now and then, when we've been inclined to break the rules to advance our careers or cover our hind parts.

Others, of course, make cheating a way of life, and contrasting ourselves to them may give us false comfort. After all, we think, those who live by the sword also die by it. On the other hand, a friend of mine who was at the top of his giant corporation, and in the running for the CEO position, committed one major indiscretion and was fired. Though overall he behaved ethically, after his one misstep he languishes in self-doubt with his career a shambles.

TAKE ACTION

1. Guard against cynicism. Tote up the majority of projects you're engaged in where you cooperate with your associates more than you compete with them.
2. Don't be tempted to break the rules. If that's required to win at what you're doing, you're in the wrong game. Not the wrong company, necessarily, but the wrong game.

22

MOVING TOWARD PEOPLE

Q: **Have you been criticized
by associates and subordinates
for isolating yourself from
them?**

A: Usually/Often _____
Sometimes/Seldom _____

Y ESTERDAY I HAD lunch with a client of mine who is vice president of executive and organizational development for his large corporation. His job is loaded with challenges, and he makes the most of it. His charter is nothing less than designing opportunities for executives to increase their competence and self-esteem, and, therefore, his corporation's performance.

He's the right person for that job. He grew up under a strong father who founded and ran a successful family business. Throughout his youth he showed outstanding leadership potential, and his father looked forward to his taking over the business someday.

In his sophomore year in college, he told his father that his plans for his life did not include joining the family business. His father flew into a rage, disowned him, and cut off all funding. The young man got a loan from a friend, bummed around Europe for a year, and eventually settled in the Bahamas. There he joined an office supply company, and for three years was its top salesman. On the side, he taught an English literature course for seniors in a Catholic high school in Nassau.

Late one night, walking alone on the beach, he was "seized," as he puts it, with a deep sense of loneliness. It was for him a crisis of spirit, and it began his trek back.

He left the islands, and with the money he'd saved, paid off his friend's loan and completed college. This was the late 1960s, and while on campus, he became a long-haired moderate leader in the peace movement.

He's since trimmed his locks, of course, and today you'll find him in exemplary business dress rather than bib overalls, but he dates his concern for a commitment to developing people back to that night on the beach when he was overcome by a sense of isolation.

Integrating Ideas

I think it's nifty as hell that this outstanding corporation's executive development activities are performed by a person who has at his inner core a concern for the isolation that people allow in their lives.

We allow isolation not only among ourselves, but also among ideas that ought to be integrated. For instance, it may seem odd to you that I'm treating a subject that pertains to management in a vein that's spiritual. Yet isn't it true that an executive who habitually seals himself off from others either physically (behind closed doors and a legion of secretaries) or emotionally (with aloofness and a lack of candor) is setting himself up for loneliness of the heart? The answer to *this* question is obviously yes, making it clear why the answer to the opening question should be "sometimes/seldom."

The Ties That Bind

We often forget the starkly simple idea that a corporation is nothing more than an *inter*-personal network with prescribed tasks, and when the *inter* breaks down, so does the corporation. The ties that bind are no less necessary here than they are for a family, university, hospital, religious institution, neighborhood, or army.

TAKE ACTION

1. Ask yourself: Am I unreachable to people? Do I isolate myself by moving away from them, or distance myself by moving against them?
2. If you do either habitually, pledge to reestablish contact with those with whom you share tasks by moving toward them. This will put you on the team, and that's where your organization needs to have you.

23

LIKE NO OTHER PERSON

Q: **Do you seize opportunity, rather than waiting for it to knock?**

A: Usually/Often _____
Sometimes/Seldom _____

T HERE'S A MAN who used to work at NBC-TV that Jane Pauley called a volcano. Tom Brokaw said he should never be allowed to talk into a newsman's ear, because when he does, it comes right out the other side. Yet Bryant Gumbel said he's one of those rare people we all envy because he does for a living what really makes him happy.

The man is Steve Friedman, former producer of the *Today* show. Industry gossip says he had a falling out with Bryant Gumbel. In 1987, as soon as he left, he teamed up with Grant Tinker, former CEO of NBC, as East Coast president of Tinker's GTG Entertainment.

In spite of his volatility, Friedman's success in his seven-year tenure was spectacular. With him as its producer, *Today* knocked off front-runner *Good Morning America* and reached the point where it was pouring $20 million annually into NBC's coffers.

Friedman's philosophy is to hire the smartest people he can find and let them do their jobs. As for the demands he makes on himself, *Rolling Stone* quoted him as saying:

> Go with your gut, take a stand, be smart, don't blame others, be together. When it succeeds, there's plenty of room for everybody. When it fails, no one's safe. When you have the lead, you can try to do more things. If we have a bad segment, who cares? The key element is to gamble. Roll the dice. We'll have more ambitious trips, and we'll do things to bust the format.

The Times Making Man

Had Einstein been born in Brazil in 1750, we might not know about him, and someone else would have discovered that $E = mc^2$. FDR thought years before our entry into World War II that this would be required of us. But it was not until Japan's attack on Pearl Harbor that he was able to rally the support of the American people for the war effort.

In his latter days at Ford, Lee Iacocca was banished to a warehouse, where he wept, wailed, gnashed his teeth, and, by his own admission, drank too much. The times arose at Chrysler, though, when what he had to give was exactly what the doctor ordered. He'd had a distinguished career at Ford, but at Chrysler he soared. Yes, he saved a company, but a company also saved him.

These are examples of the times making people.

Man Making the Times

I believe that history and careful observation show that the times make people more often than vice versa. Yet there are great hordes who exist in times of opportunity and don't give what they have to offer that would be valued. Those who do, in their small way, are people who make the times.

There's a piece of wisdom captured in a little trilogy that bears repeating to yourself: (1) I'm like all other people; (2) I'm like some other people; (3) I'm like no other person. The one who gives to his organization what is *distinctively him*—the way he is like no other person—will produce results his associates think impossible. For such people, the answer to the question is "usually/often."

Steve Friedman gives what is distinctively him. Says he: "I don't worry about keeping my job. I worry about doing it."

TAKE ACTION

1. Acknowledge what is *distinctively you*.
2. Find a way to give it, right where you are.

24

MESHULAM'S RULE

Q: **Do you treat every piece of paper in your in-box as being of equal importance?**

A: Usually/Often _____
Sometimes/Seldom _____

ONE OF THE most shrewd, flamboyant characters in big corporate America is Meshulam Riklis. Riklis isn't a chief executive type. He's above that. He's an *owner*. He *hires* chief executives. Born in Turkey in 1923, he came to this country in 1947 as a high school graduate with an interest in mathematics, barely able to speak English. He graduated from Ohio State with a B.A. in 1950. He eventually earned his M.B.A. there as well in 1966. Riklis began his career as a researcher and stockbroker in 1951 with Piper, Jaffray & Hopwood in Minneapolis. On the side, he taught courses on the Torah in a local Hebrew school.

By 1960 he had catapulted himself to vice chairman of McCrory Corp., the retail chain. By 1970 he was chairman of Rapid-American Corporation, a conglomerate he put together that included McCrory, Glen Alden (a distilled beverages company), and Playtex International, with combined annual sales over $1 billion.

He wore full-length fur coats. He divorced his wife and married Pia Zadora, a café singer whom critics used to lambaste at every turn. He's ruthless, but also charming. He laughs easily, likes to have a good time, and gives entertaining speeches. I heard him address a group of thin-lipped financial analysts at the height of the "funny money" days in 1969. "All that matters," he said, "is P/E and PR." You had to be there, but believe me, he brought the house down.

Years later, in an interview with a newsweekly, he got to talking about the mail he receives in business. In his usual outrageous style, he said something like, "I don't read it. I let it age for six months. When I get to it, it doesn't need any attention."

Riklis Is Right

Meshulam's "Rule of Correspondence" is exaggerated, of course, but makes its point. Much of the paper that flows incessantly across our desks is distracting at worst or meaningless at best.

Surely we can't ignore it, but neither can we afford to dote over it, handling and rehandling it.

I've learned that, by and large, good news comes by telephone, bad news by mail. I know that checks, signed contracts, acceptances from Yale, love letters, coveted reports, and the like go out through the mail, but most often people like to deliver good news face to face, and if they are prohibited by geography, then voice to voice.

Whether it comes under Uncle Sam's auspices or intracompany, most mail is routine or of secondary importance. This is all the more reason for realizing that the answer to the question should be "sometimes/seldom."

Paper Shuffling and People

The purpose of setting priorities with our in-boxes is to have more time where it counts: with people, face-to-face, voice-to-voice, dealing with the good news, and even those pieces of mail that do matter the most.

Exchanging ideas, acknowledging what we don't know, forming opinions, learning facts, making presentations, debating points of view, discovering opportunities, offering encouragement, generating alternatives, facing rivalries, calling a spade a spade, and yes, even admitting defeat—this and much, much more, is the good news of hands-on management. It is collaboration.

TAKE ACTION

1. When it comes to your in-box, do it now or let it age.
2. When it comes to aging, don't follow Meshulam's rule. Six months is too long and makes a shambles of your office. One month should do it.

25

GETTING OUT OF THE MIND'S WAY

Q: Do you neglect to set aside large blocks of time to do creative work and planning?

A: Usually/Often _____
Sometimes/Seldom _____

As I WRITE this, I'm sitting aboard American Airlines Flight 277. We're taxiing at New York's La Guardia Airport, about to take off for Chicago. It's Friday night and the workweek's over. I've loosened my tie, I've unbuttoned my collar, and I'm looking forward to the flight.

The reason I'm looking forward to this flight is not just because it's Friday night and I'm heading home. No, I'm savoring it because I like to fly. And I like to fly because I believe I do some of my best thinking in the air. This two-hour trip, for instance, will give me enough time to organize my thoughts on the subject at hand.

With no telephone to interrupt, no appointments to keep, no conferences to attend, and a window seat that takes me out of the action as much as possible, I'm able to cast my thoughts in a useful direction.

I find it exceedingly difficult to carve out this kind of hassle-free time in the office. Not only do the operating necessities of phone, meetings, and the rest impose themselves, but the mere *trappings* of business assault my brain in wraparound sound and fury, reminding me of tasks undone, questions not answered, options not discussed, trips yet to be scheduled, agendas yet to be set. The props are all there, and I can't help but use them. You see what I mean, I'm sure. Try not thinking of the color blue when I say to you, "Don't think of the color blue."

As I'm sure you've guessed by now, the answer to the question should be "sometimes/seldom."

Solitude and Reflection

Most executives know down deep that they neglect giving themselves respite from the battle. Yet when they finally remove themselves from the roar, or events simply conspire to make that happen, they are forced to admit how very useful the respite is.

Case in point: I've noticed that many executives approach their jobs with added vigor and imagination at the first of each year. This is just as true, by the way, for executives whose companies operate on a fiscal-year basis as for those on the calendar year. In other words, their zest has nothing to do with their *business* starting anew.

Rather, the source of their freshness is time spent collecting their thoughts over the holidays. If I've heard one executive say something like, "Over the holidays I got this idea . . . ," I've heard a thousand.

The Purpose

The purpose of chunks of time away from the workplace is not "rest and recreation," although they inevitably occur as by-products. Rather, the purpose is to get all the clutter out of your mind's way, to let *it* play and entertain notions not accommodated in the heat of battle.

The result of time spent in solitude and reflection is the rediscovery of what is *distinctively you*, what you believe in, and what you believe you can bring to fruition. That's what your company needs from you. That's your contribution.

TAKE ACTION

1. Find a time when you can be alone. Make it regular.
2. Name a place where you can get everything out of your mind's way. Backyard. Beach. Basement. Go there!

26

OWNING UP
TO IGNORANCE

Q: **Is it difficult for you to
admit to your associates
that you are ignorant
about a subject?**

A: Usually/Often _____
Sometimes/Seldom _____

In an earlier day, "ignorance" included the idea of willfulness. It simply meant the state of ignoring facts one ought to heed. It doesn't seem to mean that anymore, at least in the way most of us use the word. Today, ignorance typically refers to a lack of knowledge of an area or field. In the past, to call people ignorant was to deride them flatly. But now it is common—and often desirable—for us to own up to our ignorance. However, a twist on that early definition applies to some executives today who, to their detriment, routinely refuse to admit to a lack of knowledge. These executives ignore their own ignorance.

The Know-It-All

Such a person's self-image is so underdeveloped that he acts with bloated ambition. Even with the expansion of knowledge that we've experienced at an exponential rate, he won't bring himself to tell his associates that he's inexperienced and unknowing in the face of some new undertaking. He thinks that to do so would be to display some fatal flaw, to admit that he hasn't mastered what he assumes great people master. But since he wants to be great, yet senses in his innards that he isn't, he pretends to omniscience. Just being "normal" with limitations of knowledge and experience isn't good enough. Such a person assures his failure because his phantoms of knowledge exist only in his own mind, and his associates shun working with him in any meaningful way. Some try to help him see the error of his ways, while others merely let him hang himself, primarily because he seems closed to help. He bristles or withdraws when it is offered.

True, this picture is extreme. Yet in small measure, this is what we all do when, in our occasional lapses into human perversity, we claim to know something we don't. With relief, I say that the answer to the above question should be "sometimes/seldom."

The Sharer of Ignorance

How much more healthful it is to share ignorance! While it's bad form not to know what you clearly should, it's no shame fessing up to not knowing something you'd like to know or need to know. This is a means of identifying what you have yet to grasp in order to excel.

The modern world of work requires the sharing of ignorance in exchange for the sharing of knowledge. Most of what gets done in today's complex organizations—whether in corporations, universities, hospitals, communities, religious institutions, or whatever—is accomplished through collaboration and joint effort. For such work groups to be effective in dealing with inevitable evolutionary change and new projects, they have to direct their discussions and analysis to what they don't know. This is essential for identifying what needs to be mastered, and determining margins of error and probabilities for what cannot be mastered, learned, or even identified.

TAKE ACTION

1. Ruminate a bit. Take out pen and paper and jot down five instances in the past year when you have claimed among your work associates that you knew more than you did. If one or two of these were calculated bluffs and spurs to later making good on your claims, that's OK. If more than that, you're jeopardizing your performance and career.
2. List five areas of ignorance you need to share with your work associates and have them make lists of their own. Everyone should share these lists at a group meeting. People will likely say such things as, "Aw, you know more about that than you think," or "Yes, I agree that you're a bit shaky there. I'd be glad to coach you on that if you'll coach me on this." The meeting is likely to result in more positive teamwork.

27

THE RISK OF BRAINSTORMING

Q: **Do you consider brainstorming with your associates a waste of time?**

A: Usually/Often _____
Sometimes/Seldom _____

THERE ARE MANY executives who right off the bat will tell you they have no time for brainstorming. They say it is ineffective. Others say they avoid brainstorming whenever they can because its setting and process make them uneasy. Their reasons appear to be based on emotional discomfort more than the former group's. Yet it becomes clear with some probing that the concerns of both are pretty much the same.

Spurned Thoughts and Wasted Efforts

When an executive gives what he considers hard, honest thoughts in a free-wheeling problem-solving session—only to have them rejected in favor of an idea or ideas from some other quarter—it's easy to see how he thinks he's been wasting his time, and also feels intensely uncomfortable.

He considers the process ineffective because the idea that was adopted could have been advanced without his being present, and he could have been giving his time and effort to something else. He also suffers emotional discomfort (though he may not admit it to himself) because he feels devalued. In short, he concludes that his ideas weren't good enough.

We all have been in this executive's shoes, so nobody's making any judgment here. But this simple example does show how we misunderstand the purpose of the collaborative process and are inclined to be a bit vain.

First off, the idea that gets adopted usually does not emerge without the mixing and contrasting of all kinds of ideas, including our own. We have to be there, participating.

Second, desiring that we be habitually "first among equals" is hardly a noble or mature sentiment and, moreover, assures our failure.

Fear of Uncertainty

You may have heard the story of a man standing in the shadows beneath a streetlamp staring intently into the gutter for money he'd lost. A passerby stopped to find out what he was doing, and when he learned, asked, "Well, just where did you lose it?" The man replied, "Oh, up the block a ways." The startled passerby blurted, "Then why for heaven's sake are you looking here?" The man answered, "Because the light's better!"

Our wish for clarity and certainty sometimes prompts us to pursue activities that are sideshows rather than main events, that provide answers to questions no one is asking, and solutions to problems that are secondary. Many of us would rather make minor decisions our way than participate in brainstorming to make major decisions.

However, when responsive executives encounter an unanticipated problem in a critical area, they usually are required to face it squarely in a collaborative, problem-solving discipline that involves four steps: (1) clarifying the problem, (2) formulating alternatives, (3) predicting consequences of the alternatives, and (4) choosing an alternative.

This brainstorming process is a "buck stops here" activity loaded with uncertainty and, therefore, risk. That risk is not only corporate, but personal. The participants are associated with the outcome.

Yet living well with such uncertainty is essential if anyone is to be an achiever. This makes the better answer to the question "sometimes/seldom."

TAKE ACTION

1. Count the events in the past year when you wanted to be "first among equals." Look and laugh at them. Laugh easily with yourself about how grand you were!
2. Identify and eliminate (or at least downplay) the sideshows in which you're engaged. Then spend your time and effort on what needs help. This is what makes you valuable and places you on center stage.

28

ON BEING
A CLARINET

Q: **Do your associates think you're thin-skinned?**

A: Usually/Often _____
Sometimes/Seldom _____

YOU'VE HEARD THE expression: "You had to be there!" It certainly applies to an occasion I'm going to describe, so I won't try to capture its humor. But I want to tell you about it nonetheless.

A few friends and I were sitting around one early afternoon not too long ago with a handful of jazz musicians. We all were listening to a top-notch storyteller, John Coppola, and he had us in the palm of his hand.

Coppola is a San Francisco bandleader and a fine, fine trumpet player in his own right. He's played with some of the great bands, and on this occasion was telling us about an experience he had playing for Benny Goodman, the "king of swing," who died recently.

" 'Somethin's wrong with the song,' says Goodman in rehearsal, glowering at the band. 'Let's try it again, but Coppola, I wanna hear just your part.' I reply, 'What part? It's two notes!' 'Play it,' says Goodman, and starts tapping his foot, sounding like a fast drip of a leaky faucet: dit-dit-dit-dit-dit dit-dit-BLIP-dit-dit-BLIP. At each BLIP, he points at me and I blow.

"Goodman exclaims, 'That's it, Your notes don't swing. Make 'em swing!' Everybody in the band roars." So did we. Coppola then turned to us and said, "Y'know, Goodman stopped being a human being when he was around eight years old. That's when he turned into a clarinet." We roared again.

The Extra Dimension

By telling this story on himself, Coppola won our respect. We already knew he was a first-rate musician, but if we hadn't, the fact that he qualified for Goodman's band would have told us so. This was a story of a good man telling us how he got better.

Absorption with our craft and not being thin-skinned are what this story is about. Had Coppola bristled and sulked over Goodman's abstruse criticism of his playing, he would have prevented himself from acquiring that extra little something that enriched his performance.

Whenever we come upon people who are particularly good at what they do, we always find that they were exposed to a master teacher of some sort. Not necessarily a mentor, mind you, but somebody they could learn from, if by no other means than merely watching them.

Absorption With Our Craft

Actually, Coppola's tag line offers the biggest lesson for us all. When actors begin their training, they are given nonhuman roles to play. Imagine being a house. How would you enact that? Or a car? Or a river?

How would an IBM salesman's performance be affected if he practiced being a computer? Or an auto supply salesman's if he practiced being a wrench? Or a financial analyst's if she practiced being a return on investment? Well . . . loony as this may sound, Coppola's point is that when Benny Goodman played he *was* a clarinet. And anybody that good *is what he does* and is open to suggestion and observations from others because of his commitment to superior performance.

This means that the answer to the question should be "sometimes/seldom."

TAKE ACTION

1. Ask and answer whether you have lost the respect of some of your associates because you refuse criticism.
2. If you have, go to one of them, acknowledge your thin skin, and offer your thanks for that person's interest. This is a start.

29

THE STRENGTH OF VULNERABILITY

Q: **Do you have a confidant or two in your company with whom you share your most candid thoughts and emotions?**

A: Usually/Often _____
Sometimes/Seldom _____

A SCHOLAR I admire and pay attention to perhaps more than any other is Peter Berger. Berger is University Professor and Director of the Institute for the Study of Economic Culture at Boston University. His main discipline is sociology, and I became acquainted with his work when I was a fledgling college professor in 1963.

I used his classic book *Invitation to Sociology* for a seminar I taught that year and came upon his statement that only geniuses and psychotics can get along without approval of others.

Despite my reverence for Berger, I doubted at the time that geniuses were exempt from this most human of all needs, and not too long ago, I learned it isn't even true of psychotics.

I was at the side of a friend who is a clinical psychologist. He invited me to sit in with him on some of his consultations with clients in a nearby residential mental health facility. One client, apparently not on the same wavelength as most of us, was doing his utmost by way of antics and unintelligible language to have us absolutely certain of it.

At one point, however, my friend the doctor waved the patient away, dismissing him from the counseling room with the words, "Oh . . . go be schizophrenic somewhere else!"

The words of the doctor struck home, and there was a flicker of deep hurt on the client's face before he got up and stormed out of the room in anger. If I didn't know it before, I knew it then: *Everybody* needs approval.

The Bully

There's a person in the executive suite we're also tempted to think doesn't need approval, and that's the bully. Bullies project a menacing presence with their loud voices, incriminating questions, arched eyebrows, swagger, ever-ready threats, and traveling cast of hand-picked sycophants in order to convince all onlookers of their raw, undisputed power. They also shoot the messenger who brings the bad news.

Actually, the bully feels most helpless of us all. Like the client storming out of the room, he's hurting and concocts the blustering and elaborate orderliness of control in his life and work to mask—most of all from himself—his sense of inadequacy. He can't be satisfied with ordinary human accomplishment and limitations, so he becomes superhuman—but only in his own mind. In the process, he becomes less than human, and, eventually, a dismal failure.

Inviting Attack

The bully makes himself a fortress, and a fortress makes attack irresistible. There is always some Joshua with his trumpet who'll make those walls come tumbling down.

We need each other. Rather than being an isolated bully, or wishing we had the supposed power of one, it is much more healthful and constructive to be vulnerable by acknowledging our dependence on others, having our ideas checked by those we trust and our concerns listened to by those who care about us.

I'm not asking you to be indiscreet or maudlin. Pick your times, places, and people very carefully. But pick them nonetheless. The answer to the question should be "usually/often."

TAKE ACTION

1. Recognize that you can't go it alone. There's no future for the lone traveler.
2. Show your courage and build your strength by admitting your mistakes and asking advice.

30

THE GADFLY'S VANITY

Q: **Are you eager to be the messenger who brings bad news to the boss?**

A: Usually/Often _____
Sometimes/Seldom _____

THERE'S A ONE-LINER we sometimes use to put bigmouths in their places. The first time I heard it, I was a high school baseball player sitting on the bench with our team at bat. Our coach—ever voluble and contentious—had just sprung from our bench to contest an "out" call at first base by the umpire.

He often blew up at what he perceived as unjust judgments, and we on the team had settled into expecting his frequent tangling with the game's final decision maker. We accepted it as part of a coach's job—or at least as part of the way *this* coach understood his job.

On this particular occasion, however, in the midst of our coach quarreling with the ump—heatedly calling the latter's intelligence and ability into question—a powerful voice came from one of the fans in the stands behind us, shouting the one-liner I mentioned that delighted everyone watching the game: "Tell him all you know, Jack, it'll only take a minute!"

The explosive laughter prompted throughout the stadium by this biting remark was a curtain to the drama at first base, and the argument was over.

Just like that.

The New Broom

A management career is over too, just like that, when some indefinable point is reached in a company and an executive is labeled a *gadfly*. History may be forgiving of gadflies, as in the case of Socrates, but the present is not. Gadflies are "put in their places" just as surely as our coach was with the thrust of this one word.

We are in awe of frontier people, those who display their courage by risking life, limb, and psyche by charting unknown lands and facing assorted dangers. Likewise, we embarrassedly acknowledge the wisdom of the little one who—unlike us—freely exclaims that the emperor has no clothes.

On the other hand, the gadfly eventually grows irksome to

us and is heroic mainly in his own mind. Though it's a truism that there are times when we all shirk our responsibility to speak up on risky causes, believe it or not, the gadfly *loves* to deliver bad news to the boss.

The gadfly most often is the new broom that sweeps clean. When he first joins the company, everybody says, "Oh, isn't this terrific. He's so refreshing. He's not afraid to speak his mind." Later, it begins to dawn on people that he *always* speaks his mind, and he's more concerned with getting attention by stirring the pot than with what's actually being stirred.

Sifting Priorities

Whereas the gadfly never suffers from having an unexpressed thought, the executive who can point to a steady, lifelong career of accomplishment is one who has sorted out what he believes in most deeply and takes a stand on it.

This assures a positive, proactive posture toward one's work, and means that one's efforts are devoted to making things go right, rather than to pointing out what's going wrong.

When you set your priorities carefully from among all the tasks that could assault your energies, you'll be prepared and convincing on those few occasions when your convictions require your differing with your boss. This is why the answer to the question should be "sometimes/seldom."

TAKE ACTION

1. Don't be a gadfly. Sure, speak up if you feel that something is very important, but this should not be your central role. Leave the picky whining to the losers.
2. Scan all that's going on in your enterprise. Get clear

about what you believe in and can assist with. Pay attention to that rather than being tempted by constantly finding fault. Then you'll discover how much more you have in common with your boss than the ways in which you differ. This won't make you a sycophant. It will make you a contributor.

31

A KEEPER
IS A FIND

Q: **Do your associates seek
you out for collaboration
on projects?**

A: Usually/Often _____
Sometimes/Seldom _____

COLLABORATION IS TODAY'S premier management style. Even with the call for leadership whirling all around us, and the Iacoccas conjuring up an image of a present-day General Patton striding about the executive suite, the most critical decisions made and most effective actions taken in our corporations come about in a setting most accurately described as collaborative. More than ever, managers huddle, and they do so because they believe two or more heads are better than one. The answer to the question, then, should be "usually/often." Make sure this is true of your work life.

Sought, Not Tolerated

Some people make a career of just *sort of* being there. They just hang around, part of the landscape, but are not thought of as being indispensable in any way. It's true that no one is literally indispensable, but we all want to qualify as a "keeper."

A keeper, according to one company president whom I know, is any executive on his team who makes a vital contribution. For him, a keeper is someone whom he must not let get away. And even in a severe economic downturn, when other executives might be given their walking papers, a keeper is retained.

A keeper, obviously, is not a nebbish who is tolerated for doing a good enough job, but rather someone who makes things happen, and whose ideas, opinions, and efforts are sought by associates on a regular basis. "Be sure to run that idea past Tom." "I wouldn't dream of taking on this project unless we can get Kim to be part of it. She's got a knack for this. She sees things the rest of us don't see!" These are the kinds of words spoken about keepers.

Seeking, Not Excluded

Keepers, then, are collaborators. They're givers, not takers. They're givers of self. What leads to being sought for collaboration, ironically, is *seeking* collaboration by volunteering your own. You know the old saying: "If you want to get letters, you have to send them."

During the 1960s and 1970s in this country, we heard an awful lot about various groups of people being alienated. And we often heard this vocabulary drifting into the corporate world where individuals referred to themselves as being alienated from this or that group of power or influence.

Do you hear the passivity and withholding of self in the phrase "being alienated"? How much more important it is to seize initiative, and give the gifts of self, to avoid being left out of the circles of power and influence. In most cases, in the executive suite, people are not alienated. They alienate.

TAKE ACTION

1. Write down three circumstances in the past year when you sat by idly in meetings and let someone else speak up with an idea or opinion that was similar to your own, but that person got credit that could have gone to you. Vow to strike that passivity from your demeanor. You'll thrive on your new-found energy, and your associates will be gratified at your contribution.

2. Look around you today in your department and identify some project under way—or one in its planning stages— that you care about. Jump in. Have a stake in it by volunteering your views. Make a habit of this, and you'll be sought for collaboration regularly. You'll become a keeper.

32

DEALING YOURSELF IN

Q: **Do you volunteer your services as a collaborator on projects when you haven't been asked?**

A: Usually/Often _____
Sometimes/Seldom _____

DESPITE THEIR JAM-PACKED schedules, most accomplished executives find it difficult to turn down a request for their efforts on some project—even though they aren't part of it. On the other hand, it is the astute executive who learns when best to take initiative by offering his services on a project even though they haven't been sought.

The Caring Contribution

The "when best" is determined by the convergence of a project under way or about to be with the belief by the executive that he has something distinctive to contribute.

It is common to let those occasions pass without action from us, on the grounds that to ask to be included would make us appear audacious. Yet if we stand on the perimeter of involvement awaiting an invitation, it may well never come, and chances are we'll be left feeling like the little kid whose nose is pressed up against Macy's window at Christmas.

There are all kinds of reasons why we're not asked to be a key player on a project. One, of course, is that we're simply not wanted. Unfortunately, that's what many of us are inclined to think, and although it may be a possibility, it most often is not.

Another is that the existing project team assumes we're too concerned with our other responsibilities to give this one our attention. Another is that although we have abilities and values that would serve in support of the undertaking, we have not taken the trouble to let the relevant parties know of our interest. Still another is that unwittingly we have sent out a signal that the project is beneath us.

Winning Respect

It is our caring contribution that wins respect from associates. And it is the caring contribution that is made possible by our speaking up. It is made possible, first of all, by declaring "count me in," followed by unfiltered expression of our thoughts throughout the life of the project.

The notion of "campaign" comes to mind in this regard, along with the actions a couple of years ago by an executive I consider among the best I've been privileged to know.

The executive was senior vice president of sales of a large company known for its manufacturing sophistication. Among its recent acquisitions was a small division comprising four plants scattered throughout the United States.

Seeing potential in this division that his bosses treated as a poor relation, he went to his chairman to persuade him to let him run it. Shocked that he had any interest in this business, let alone that he was willing to give up his top sales job for it, the chairman nonetheless relented after two weeks of intense lobbying.

With an arsenal of fresh ideas, and despite a hard-won, heavy investment budget, the executive in one year made this division the company's highest-profit unit per sales dollar, and its growth potential is now apparent to all at corporate headquarters.

This story beautifully illustrates why the answer to the question should be "usually/often."

TAKE ACTION

1. Stop waiting for an invitation to do what you need to do.
2. Show interest where you have conveyed disinterest without intending to.

33

TURNING UP
THE AMPS

Q: **Do you make little-known associates into supporters by taking them into your confidence?**

A: Usually/Often _____
Sometimes/Seldom _____

Y OU'RE SITTING ALONE at a corner table in the cafeteria. You're right next to a window that looks out on the duck pond on your corporate campus. It's raining cats and dogs on the ducks, so there's not much cheer to see out there today, despite your bucolic setting.

But it's cheerful inside, because you just may have had a dandy idea while munching on that tuna salad sandwich on pasty white bread (you'd come late, so no luck on the whole wheat).

You've been paying particular attention to Steve the past few minutes. He's with some of his pals in marketing, and you can tell they're all getting ready to leave. They'll pass near your table when they walk their trays to the conveyer before going back to work, and you wonder if you should flag him down.

Steve runs market research, and there's part of your dilemma. You're in sales. Sales and marketing are supposed to be a hand-in-glove operation, but in your company, they're competitive. Those in marketing think the people in sales are the drones, while *they're* the ones with the ideas. Sales thinks the people in marketing are a bunch of pansies whose knees would quake if they ever had to look a real customer in the eye.

This stereotyped rivalry strikes you as nonsense, and you suspect Steve feels the same way. But you don't *know*. Yet you know enough about him to suspect that he's just the guy to help you design the new customer service program you're spearhead-ing—the one that's "top secret." To let someone in on it from marketing would be "treasonous."

"Steve," you beckon, "got a couple of minutes? I'd like to kick an idea around with you." That's the spirit! You know the answer to the question should be "usually/often."

Little-Known Associates

There are people we work with whom we know, whom we like and don't like, trust and don't trust. Then there are those whom we know very little, whom we don't know whether we like or not, trust or not.

In Chapter 12, I wrote about working for a bad boss, how almost everyone has to go through such an experience, and that a sign of a career-long winner is someone making good in such a circumstance. In the chapter before that, I urged you to be prepared to work for a boss who would tax your total capacities. But here the focus is on people in your organization with whom you've been at some distance; with whose work, attitude, and style you are only smatteringly familiar. Yet you get good vibes.

Make Them Supporters

Trust your intuition. Even though for now, pertaining to you, that person may have the mark of neutrality stamped on his forehead, it can be erased with a small spurt of initiative on your part.

Small, but not inconsequential. And not lacking in judgment born of reflection. When our hypothetical hero seized Steve in the cafeteria, his action wasn't as spontaneous as it seemed. He knew risks were involved in sharing his idea, but he'd been keeping his eye on Steve in joint department meetings and believed that Steve would get behind him.

TAKE ACTION

1. Avoid stereotyped thinking. Be alert to people you don't rub shoulders with who might have something to give to your projects.
2. Test your intuition with a little time. See if those good vibes are capable of great amplitude.

34

TEMPERING YOUR TRUST

Q: **Do you worry about trusting people too much?**

A: Usually/Often _____
Sometimes/Seldom _____

I WAS NEWLY married and in my mid-twenties. My wife and I were thinking about starting our family. I was a graduate student, making big plans, full of big ideas. Graduate students are like that.

Over coffee one afternoon in my school's commons, a fellow student and I conversed. He too was newly married, and we were exchanging big ideas on raising children.

He was a commuter student and told me a story about his next-door neighbor in the suburb where he lived. The neighbor was a few years older than we and was the father of a three-year-old son.

One day the father stood on the ground and watched while his son climbed up and stood on the railing to the back porch of their house. The boy's feet were about level with his father's head. The father beckoned to his son, asking him to jump, and he would catch him. The son was doubtful about all this, but after a short pause, jumped. His father stood aside and made no attempt to catch his son, so that the boy tumbled to the ground. He wasn't hurt at all, but was stunned, looked up at his father, and began to cry.

The father bent over, picked up his son, and hugged him. When the boy stopped crying, he said to him: "Son, it's a nasty world out there, and I want you to learn you can't trust anybody."

Being Let Down

This story made me shudder in the retelling here even more than it did the first time I heard it. The well-intentioned father might have his supporters, but it seems likely that his actions were more a predictor of what his relations with his son would become, rather than successful radical training for living.

I once had a strong mentor relationship with a talented young executive. This man sought my counsel at many points, and I gladly gave it, taking pleasure in the warmth of our friendship and the ability he applied to his tasks. A mutual acquaintance of ours, one of his peers, warned me of this man's ambitions and said for me to be careful, that he would let me down eventually.

As with the errant father, this was well-intentioned but faulty advice.

Expecting Too Much

Of course the young executive let me down, just as *I* have let any number of people down with my actions. Yet our friendship remains strong, as I've foresaken the role of mentor and become a sometimes-sparring, full-fledged peer. No patronizing. Few obligations.

The "few obligations" means I don't expect too much from my friend. I know what I can count on him for and what I can't. In this way, I've tempered my trust. To be sure, he sometimes disappoints me, but oh, brother, in most areas, does he deliver the goods!

Yet the point to keep in mind is that almost everybody who's important to us on our jobs is worthy of at least *contingent* trust. Acknowledging the occasions for such trust allows us to answer the question "sometimes/seldom."

TAKE ACTION

1. Be sensitive to others' needs. Put yourself into their shoes. Why should they trust *you*? Then ask yourself if what you want from them in the way of trust violates their prior loyalties to other people and priorities. If this is the case, you're expecting too much.
2. Don't be once-burned, twice-shy. Be wary, to be sure, but don't allow yourself to be callous. Live forward, not backward.

35

TAKING INITIATIVE ON TRUST

Q: **Do your associates think you're not trusting enough of others?**

A: Usually/Often _____
   Sometimes/Seldom _____

I WAS A freshman in college and just settled into my dormitory with my roommate. Right across the hall were two guys, one of whom I liked instantly, the other of whom I backed away from. Over the first semester, this latter fellow and I were thrown together by happenstance and became the best of friends. The next semester *we* became roommates.

In graduate school, I served an internship as a counselor at a training school for boys the court had judged as delinquent. My boss was someone I didn't like. In the six short months I worked for him, he taught me tons, had a lifelong impact on me, and earned my liking as well as my admiration.

When I launched my own consulting firm in 1969, one of my first clients was someone I didn't trust. She was abrasive and sought every opportunity to ridicule my performance. I did my job but remained wary. Yet our working relationship grew and lasted ten years until she retired. The extensive exposure I received from her at the highest levels in the magazine publishing industry was one of the most important influences in my adult professional life.

The late Marshall McLuhan wrote, "War is education." "What an odd statement," I thought. Then I remembered some studies from World War II that showed how prejudice of whites against blacks disappeared when they shared foxholes, and the statement didn't seem odd at all.

Dislike

Sometimes it's almost laughable the way we meet people in the most trivial to the most trying circumstances and make instantaneous judgments about them. And am I right? Those judgments take the form of "I like" or "I don't like." Then it isn't far to the next conclusion: "I trust" or "I don't trust."

There's nothing wrong with acknowledging your genuine feelings about people when you first meet them. After all, what you feel is what you feel. But I've found it's instructive to go a little deeper into the sources of my immediate dislike for someone.

Does she speak with fluency and I feel tongue-tied in her presence? Is he smart and I'm dumb? Is she beautiful and I'm plain? Is he accomplished and I'm a failure? Is she charming and I'm a log? These are some of the distortions we cook up not to like somebody.

Then there are more legitimate concerns: Does her energy show up my laziness? Does his forthrightness show up my sneakiness? Does her poise show up my unwillingness to drill? And so on.

Learning to Like

There *are* people *not* to trust. No argument; they'll do you in if they can. But those situations are rare. On the other hand, learning to like people you immediately dislike leads to trust and is among life's greatest growth experiences.

My experience is that dislike is usually mutual, and (surprise, surprise) the other person feels something in us to envy as much as we find such in him. If we take the initiative to get through this discomfort and extend an open hand, we can make an ally out of an opponent, a win-win out of a lose-lose. This is why the answer to the question should be "sometimes/seldom."

TAKE ACTION

1. Don't retreat from someone for whom you have an immediate dislike. Give the relationship a chance. You may find a friend cloaked as an enemy. Trust can emerge in unlikely places.
2. Ask yourself whether your dislike and distrust come from feeling inadequate in that person's presence. If this is so, perhaps he's been a mirror and shown you a part of yourself that needs your attention. It may not feel good, but see it as a favor.

36

THINKERS
AND DOERS

Q: Do you believe your
subordinates think you
welcome new ideas and
initiatives from them?

A: Usually/Often _____
Sometimes/Seldom _____

 THE RELATIONSHIP BETWEEN bosses and their subordinates is tricky. Maintaining company controls and meeting a department's objectives while enhancing a subordinate's growth—this can tax the resources of even the best boss. Nowhere is this more apparent than in his responsibility to stimulate the best efforts of his subordinates.

A Double Perception

Right off the bat, the question introduces a key issue in this relationship: clear signals. It asks about a double perception: Do you *believe* your subordinates *think* . . . ? See what I mean by tricky? What seems so simple, simply isn't.

As a boss, consider these possibilities:

1. You believe your subordinates think you welcome new ideas and initiatives, and they do.
2. You believe they think you welcome such, but they don't.
3. You believe they don't think you welcome such, but they do.
4. You believe they don't think you welcome such, and they don't.
5. You believe they do or don't think you *usually* welcome such, but on a particular project you believe they do or don't think this, and they either do or don't.

I've ignored the whole subject of whether what you believe is actually the case, assuming that if you acknowledge all these possibilities, you're likely to manage by the maxim: "Know thyself and thy subordinates' thoughts."

The overall lesson is clear: ambiguity is inevitable in corporate communications, but with *your* subordinates, make sure the message sent is the message received.

Therefore, the answer to the question should be "usually/often." It corresponds most closely with Possibility 1.

New Ideas and Initiatives

With the ambiguity problem addressed, the more important challenge to consider is convincing subordinates that you truly welcome ideas and initiatives. And that you do so in a way that their efforts are most useful.

The most captivating way is to be a model to them as both a thinker and doer. Nobel prize–winning French philosopher Henri Bergson said it best: "Think like a man of action, act like a man of thought." There is no better advice for anyone to follow anytime, anywhere.

Many people box themselves in as either thinkers or doers, good with ideas, but not initiatives, or vice versa. To make it to the top of any corporation, and stay there, an executive has to be good with both.

As a boss, enhance your department's performance by showing your subordinates that for your initiatives to be effective up, down, and across the organization, they have to be well thought out. And show them that your ideas—no matter how sound and inventive—must be decisively put into action. By observing your example, these eager climbers are taught that you will appreciate the same from them.

TAKE ACTION

1. Take a long look at the five communications possibilities and acknowledge which one is most characteristic of your management style. If Possibility 5, you may be erratic and too much the do-it-yourself. If other than Possibility 1, you need to clarify what you expect from your subordinates, and know that they know.

2. Insist to them, no matter what the specific projects on which you collaborate, that these projects include quality thinking and doing. As one sitting at the head of the table, hold up your end of the bargain by being their model on this score.

37

ASSURING THE CREATIVE SPARK

Q: **Do you make room for the creative "perpetual juvenile" in the department or function you direct?**

A: Usually/Often _____
Sometimes/Seldom _____

Colorful Eric Hoffer, the late longshoreman-philosopher, left us with many penetrating notions to ponder. One of them concerned creative people, whom he distinguished from revolutionaries. He wrote,

> Both the revolutionary and the creative individual are perpetual juveniles. The revolutionary does not grow up because he cannot grow, while the creative individual cannot grow up because he keeps growing.

Childlike Vulnerability

Hoffer was not alone in his view. For a long time astute psychologists have pointed out that creative people have a childlike quality about them. And it was Jesus who taught his ever-anxious disciples that unless they became like little children they could not reach understanding.

Now I happen to believe that we all are creative, yet most of us aren't able to give expression to creativity because we have lost touch with the child in ourselves. Although that's an intriguing subject in itself, the subject here is that person with whom we are in contact or know about at work who is generally acknowledged to be creative.

Often we're embarrassed for or by this woman or man who so willingly risks being vulnerable. The idea she espouses, the experiment he enthusiastically recommends we undertake, the contrary opinion she advances freely, the oddball interpretation of events he serves up—all these, and more—while offering the possibility of peeling the scales from our eyes, nonetheless make us uncomfortable. "Shut up! What do you mean, the emperor with no clothes?"

Making Room

Small-group research has shown overwhelmingly that a group that does not share key values and membership criteria will have too much dissonance to accomplish anything worthwhile. On the other hand, that research also shows that groups that are totally *homogeneous* (what the social scientists call sameness) lack imagination and become inert. They are without spark.

It is important to remember that someone's being different, a dissenter, or simply outspoken is no guarantee that the person is creative. But creative people will display these and other qualities from time to time. This will further mean that creative people within a group you manage will concoct a strange brew or will stir the pot.

Making room for such people is hard. They get in the way. They slow things down. They may also just waste time because some of their ideas are wide of the mark or simply impractical. In short, they're often wrong.

But they're sometimes right, and their best ideas wouldn't occur to anyone else. When this happens, they equip us with seven-league boots. This makes the better answer to the question "usually/often."

TAKE ACTION

1. Be on the lookout for creative people in your organization whom you can tap for your function. Distinguish between persons who pride themselves on quirkiness and those whose curiosity and innocence keep them growing.
2. Make room for at least one of the latter in your department. Even when they're wrong, they'll force you to think better. You'll consider alternatives you would have overlooked—alternatives that may be appropriate later, even if not appropriate when first presented.

38

SOMETIMES A GREAT NOTION

Q: Do you encourage yourself and subordinates to ask "What if?" questions?

A: Usually/Often _____
Sometimes/Seldom _____

THE HEWLETT-PACKARD people have caught my attention all fall. They've done it with their ads run on TV during Sunday afternoon pro football games. It's a "What if?" campaign.

One segment I watched recently began with a rear shot of a Corvette tooling down a lonely road, while a narrator proclaimed something like, "An idea doesn't conform to a nine-to-five schedule."

Then the driver, whose face we haven't seen, suddenly comes upon an old gas station, abruptly steers the car onto its apron, vaults out of it and up to the seated old-timer who runs the place, and crisply asks: "Phone?"

The old-timer, who doesn't see many customers, lets us know by the twinkle in his eye that he enjoys the display of energy of this young man on a mission. He points him to the phone.

The driver, we now see, is a casually dressed after-hours account representative of Hewlett-Packard, who looks as if he's on his way to a weekend retreat in the mountains or some other idyllic respite. But he's not so much in retreat that he's lost his sense of urgency for the customer. He gets his associate on the phone—who, also after hours, is eager to receive such a call—to share what just blossomed in his brain.

After briskly reviewing the customer's major resources and need, he speaks the "eureka" line that appears in all the segments, the one that fades away without completion: "Jim, what if we . . . ?" The ad viewer and potential Hewlett-Packard customer is left to complete the "What if?" out of his own current experience and conclude, "Wouldn't it be nice to have people like that working on our account?"

The "What If?" With Self

Wouldn't it be nice to have the "What if?" process at work *anywhere*? Instead, what we have in most places is kicking sand on a flower. When he was president, Lyndon Johnson used to complain publicly that he couldn't count on his cabinet and staff to bring him fresh ideas. Yet it's not difficult to understand how his domineering and ridiculing style cowed them into mental listlessness.

If you're the boss, (and who isn't the boss of something?), set an example for your associates by demonstrating that you've done your homework. Come to that next meeting you call having already completed some "What if?" thinking on your own.

The "What If?" Process With Associates

Setting an example is effective in itself. Also important is emphasizing with your subordinates and all associates that you come to the meeting not with the answers, but in the spirit of exploration and discovery—and that you expect the same from them. This can reap unexpected, extraordinary benefits. The "eureka" of the Hewlett-Packard simulation implies a mixture of carefully fostered collaboration, mutual respect, and individual responsibility. Make sure that you can answer the question "usually/often" and you'll also make sure that the simulation becomes actual in your shop.

TAKE ACTION

1. Alone, contemplate the impossible, the absurd, the unthinkable as a solution to some problem you and your associates face.
2. So it's absurd, but if you changed this one thing about it, could it just be that . . . ?

39

ON THE SAVING OF SAVIORS

Q: When you take over a new task or function, do you practice change for change's sake?

A: Usually/Often _____
Sometimes/Seldom _____

THIS MORNING I met with the chief executive of a company where I'm going to do some key search work. The meeting was arranged by the vice president of human resources so that we could become better acquainted and I would hear firsthand the man's plans for the business.

The chief executive has been with the company for two decades, but in this top spot for just under a year. He moved steadily up the rungs of the corporate ladder, and in the last few years was groomed carefully for the last step by his predecessor in the corner office.

The company itself is far and away the dominant player in its market. That market is a tough one: highly engineered products sold to manufacturers in the aerospace industry. Yet although it exists in a fast-paced, competitive arena—requiring innovation in product development and service—what strikes me most about it is its aura of orderliness. A sense of panic is noticeably absent.

Flying home, collecting my thoughts from the morning's meeting, a theme suggested itself from the orderliness of the company and my host's consistent climb to and preparedness for the job he now holds. Moreover, from the way he talked about his business, the organization, and his plans for their future, it's clear that this was a man not given to overreaction.

An Impressive Beginning

Now, no person who has been around a pace-setting company for twenty years is able to keep his faults hidden from gimlet-eyed top management. Nor is that person, no matter how skilled and bright, able to reach the top without having experienced a fair share of failures. But in prevailing, at the very least, he shows mettle and a lack of naïveté.

My point is that my client is not at all lacking in knowing what's needed, not only to keep the company competitive, but to take it into an era of expanded growth and new markets. That's what makes his comments and style so impressive. Here is a quietly aggressive man who has big plans, yet isn't trigger-happy. A man after my heart who takes no comfort in a swash-buckling style and is a believer in the true gospel: "If it ain't broke, don't fix it."

Time Is on His Side

James Thurber, the great humorist, wrote, "He who hesitates is sometimes saved." Robert Frost cautioned, "Most of the change we think we see in life is due to truths being in and out of favor." And Blaise Pascal wrote, "It is not only old and early impressions that deceive us; the charms of novelty have the same power."

My client, in the top job for a year, is just now beginning to make important moves. His stamp will come slowly, but firmly, and with it will come that often overlooked essential: the consent of the governed. Such evolutionary change is far more likely to be in tune with what constitutes the corporation's internal and external reality.

Change for change's sake is a killer. The answer to the question should be "sometimes/seldom."

TAKE ACTION

1. New on the job? Listen to your people with a third ear before you make dramatic moves. Hear what they're telling you that they don't even know they're telling you.
2. Make them a party to *constructing* all initiatives.

40

EXPERIMENTING WITH THE PEOPLE IN PLACE

Q: When you get a new job, are you inclined to bring along "star performers" who have worked for you in previous departments or companies?

A: Usually/Often _____
Sometimes/Seldom _____

THE EXECUTIVE SEARCH business is a fascinating one. Obviously, I must find it so; I've been at it as a consultant for twenty-three years and have no intention of quitting.

What's fascinating about it is not change. Our business, as far as its structure and procedures are concerned, has hardly changed at all. In fact, I'm usually at a loss when someone asks, "What's new in your business?" My reply is something like, "Oh, not much. I'm like a dentist, you know."

What provides the fascination is its arena of observation. My business is one of the greatest laboratory experiences of all time. I can't imagine any configuration of structure and events that over time approaches executive search consulting for providing as rich an opportunity—on both a broad and deep basis—to understand corporate behavior. What a microscope!

I've seen big people act small, small people act big; people about to retire bursting with imagination, people just starting out indulging in the banal; the honest and dishonest; selfless and greedy; articulate and halting; eager and timid; brainy and slow; organized and chaotic; charming and abrasive; tenacious and quitting; pompous and humble; on and on. Basically, I've seen them all.

Certain and Uncertain

Let me point out a twist in the work of search consultants you may not know: We find people for jobs, not jobs for people. Moreover, what justifies our fees as practitioners is that the executives we uncover and present to our corporate clients as candidates are accomplished in their current jobs. In other words, they're not in the market, but are reluctant candidates who are looking at our clients just as critically as they are being looked at.

All such recruits, therefore, come to the client interview only after thorough face-to-face discussion with the consultant on how they might better their careers. No matter how much the client gives assurances to the candidate he wants for the job, that candidate, no matter how capable, is stepping into a situation fraught with uncertainty. For someone who is already very successful, changing jobs presents downside risk.

Yet executives, for the most part certain of their capacities, routinely face the uncertainty and risk associated with new jobs and leave their current positions.

Trusting and Untrusting

I say "for the most part certain" because some executives try to hedge their bet of stepping into a risky new job by bringing along a "traveling support group." This is almost always a mistake. The answer to the question should be "sometimes/ seldom."

New executives have power for a time. They squander it by towing along people they trust from their prior company or department. In so doing they show that they don't trust the people already in place or, more deadly, trust *themselves* to manage them in a new situation.

How would you expect the mass of people in an organization—depreciated by these means—to act? You're right. They bide their time and withhold their best efforts until the gunslinger and pale riders are escorted out of town with double barrels at their backs.

TAKE ACTION

1. When recruited or promoted, experiment with the people already there.
2. If you *must* bring in an outsider for a key spot, make that person a stranger, not a crony.

41

MAKING THE YES DECISION

Q: **Do you avoid making yes decisions?**

A: Usually/Often _____
    Sometimes/Seldom _____

Decision making renders an executive vulnerable. That's because a decision identifies the executive with initiatives taken or not taken, and allows onlookers to pass judgment on its quality.

Seeking to escape such judgment, some executives mistakenly avoid making decisions, hoping that issues resolve themselves. This is particularly true when the issue requires a yes decision. This makes the better answer to the question "sometimes/seldom."

Missed Opportunity

The avoidance of saying yes to initiatives in order to play it safe doesn't reduce vulnerability, though many think this. The executive who leans toward saying no is risking more than the one who, after careful deliberation, says, "Let 'er rip!"

The seduction of saying no is believing that you won't be cited for failure if you refuse to embark on risky ventures. It's easy to prefer the dullness of inertia over the anxiety of chasing victory that may be elusive.

We've just completed a generation in American business when that kind of thinking was institutionalized. This was when the return-on-assets philosophy was abused by too many top executives unwilling to say yes to initiatives that, in their early years, wouldn't have brought a high return. This period was accompanied by lower levels of productivity and our missing market opportunities that were seized by committed foreign competitors.

Yes Means Commitment

Mergermania has been spawned mainly by managements believing that a better return on assets can be secured by buying companies "arrived" in a market than by investing in their own start-up businesses. Ironically, as these corporations expand to enormous proportions, most of the businesses they bought for their attractiveness don't perform as well as they did when they were freestanding.

One reason for poorer performance is that ROA philosophy governing the colossus makes investment less available for product development in the newly acquired business than for additional arrived businesses that can be bought.

But a negative judgment has come down. For example, *Forbes*, *Fortune*, *Business Week*, and *Industry Week* magazines have all had recent cover stories validating the suspicion that most mergers don't work. Moreover, businesses spun off from giant corporations for poor performance—that then thrive on their own—are giving credence to the conviction that not enough yeses have been forthcoming on the *internal* growth of our core businesses.

Making yes decisions demands the commitment of time, effort, people, and dollars. Using these resources on a venture that may not pan out is enough to give even the boldest executive palpitations. Yet this commitment has been the heart of all our great corporations.

It's always been imperative to make yes decisions. But today we need them from *you* more than ever for our back-to-basics rebuilding of American industry.

TAKE ACTION

1. Write down ten key decisions you made in the past year. Review them one by one and place a Y beside each one that was a yes decision. If you find only one or two are so marked, it's likely you're avoiding yes decisions.
2. List five key decisions you face now. Wherever a possible initiative deserves a no, don't be apologetic. However, where your stomach tells you a yes is called for, steel yourself and let 'er rip, no matter how much it scares you.

42

STIFFENING YOUR BACK

Q: Do you avoid making no decisions?

A: Usually/Often _____
Sometimes/Seldom _____

THERE'S A TALENTED rock star out there: John Mellencamp. He lives in the unlikely town of Bloomington, Indiana, and grew up 40 miles southeast in the even more unlikely town of Seymour in this high-spirited, underrated state.

Bloomington is the home of Indiana University, while Seymour—population 16,000—would probably be totally unknown to you if it weren't the lauded subject of John Mellencamp's hit record and video "Small Town."

This hit appears among a collection of other outstanding songs on his album *Scarecrow*, which, more than anything, calls attention to the plight of today's farmers. One of the album's other songs contains a refrain that speaks to the point of this chapter. It goes: "You've got to stand for somethin', or you're gonna fall for anything."

Standing for Something

There can be no right nos without good yeses. If our no decisions at work don't occur within an overall climate of affirmation, it means our companies don't have a clear sense of direction. Or if they do, we're missing it somehow.

Every company that has grown to any stature has done so because of a founder's or founders' commitment to an overwhelmingly affirmative idea. Whoever founded the company believed against all odds in a product or service; overcame the physical, psychological, and financial obstacles of such an undertaking; launched the business; hired people; brought their wares to market; and sold them.

A lesson from this is that any kind of start-up requires one big yes. If your company has lost touch with that big yes, it's in trouble. Or if the big yes is there, but you don't know what it is, *you're* in trouble. Where would John Mellencamp be if his words didn't match his music?

To achieve, we say yes first. Then, oddly enough, to nurture and protect the yes, we have to learn how and when to say no. That can be difficult, but the yes itself coaches us. To put it another way, we have to say yes to something that matters before we can say no intelligently.

Falling for Anything

What about *your* start-ups? Suppose you've said yes to some worthwhile initiative at work, and concluded early on that it was in harmony with your company's big yes. Now what do you have to say no to, to make that yes happen? Against what must you stiffen your back that you might have fallen for?

For example, suppose someone who works for you has become a personal friend but isn't cutting it. Perhaps the situation is already beginning to drag down your department, but with your plan, say, to shorten your design deadlines for the production people, this person must be confronted—reassigned, retrained, supervised more directly, or even fired. Perhaps, too, the no in this case is putting your foot down on your timidity about having the confrontation. Whatever it may be, to avoid the no is to abandon your yes. The answer to the question, therefore, should be "sometimes/seldom."

TAKE ACTION

1. Take five minutes a day over the next week to determine the major yeses of your company. Then be bold and venture its big yes.
2. Write down five nos for your own work that will serve that yes.

43

STAKING OUT THE MIDDLE GROUND

Q: Do you avoid making "that's gonna have to wait" decisions?

A: Usually/Often _____
Sometimes/Seldom _____

I ONCE CALLED ten officers of ten different companies to ask them how they mismanaged their time. I know each of them personally, so I was counting on their being straightforward with me.

They didn't let me down. For example, the vice president of human resources of a well-known company in Cleveland said, "First thing when I arrive at the office in the morning, I ask my secretary to bring me coffee, the mail, and *The Wall Street Journal*. This guarantees the day gets a fast start on me rather than the other way around."

The president of a health-care-products company in Minneapolis said, "I allow meetings to be called I don't really want or need to attend, then cancel them at the last minute, wasting not only my time, but everybody else's as well."

One of the most intriguing observations, however, came from Donald Parker, who was senior vice president of Pan Am Airways, headquartered in New York. He had been recruited to that company to head up its passenger services. Parker, a long-time client and friend, and an executive who understands the complexities of management as well as anyone I know, said this: "I'm just not tough enough at saying, 'That's gonna have to wait.'"

Needing to Be Accessible

Most of us have learned that the so-called open-door policy can be disastrous. As noted by Robert Six, late CEO of another airline (Continental), it's often "an invitation to every whiner and lackey in the place." He further said it was one of the ways a company "treats its employees like spoiled brats."

Some may find Six's attitude offensive, but I don't. For one thing, I think he's right. Second, it's common knowledge that during his long tenure, Continental Airlines was known as a sharp, high-morale organization whose standard of passenger service was the model for the entire industry. His management style worked.

Always being physically accessible to our associates isn't possible, but we also know that the closed-door policy is even a bigger disaster than the open one. There has to be some middle ground where we gladly make ourselves available to those who frankly seek our affiliation and also want us to know their thoughts.

The Middle Ground

The necessary middle ground is often staked out by a no more complicated task than being willing to say to an associate, when facing a matter jointly that just doesn't merit top priority, "That's gonna have to wait." This means that the answer to the question should be "sometimes/seldom."

When we're willing to risk the loss of popularity among our associates in this way, we not only make more time available to ourselves in the interest of more pressing projects, but we help establish an overall crispness in our organizations that forces us all to be more clear on our priorities.

TAKE ACTION

1. Be cognizant of the time demands on your boss. Show your sensitivity to them and good judgment by not making him tell you, "That's gonna have to wait."
2. Let your subordinates know what you're doing. They'll be more likely, then, to show the same maturity with you and to respect your priorities.

44

WITH A LITTLE HELP FROM YOUR FRIENDS

Q: **Do you relish the decision-making process?**

A: Usually/Often _____
Sometimes/Seldom _____

A FORMER CLIENT —owner and founder of his own company— is bright and charming. A quick wit, he was fun to work with. He saw humor in events and often kept his associates in stitches.

His was a service business, and he knew it cold. He grew up in his industry by moving up the ranks with a competitor. He performed menial tasks for customers and progressed through management to where it became clear to him that he had more imagination for running the company than his boss, the president.

Soon after that he raised capital and launched his own company. I met him when he called me in to recruit an executive vice president for his expanding business. Having completed that assignment, I got involved in others because of rapid growth and became very familiar with my client's management style.

Despite his early success, knowledge, brilliance, and charm, his style began to wear thin. I saw in it the seeds of destruction. It was his decision making. Although he saw himself as a good decision maker, I saw him as a capricious, arbitrary one. Fearless of making decisions, he in fact made too many. He was trigger-happy and made decisions this quarter that opposed those he announced the last.

So while decisive, he was without commitment to a firm strategy. A dashing captain on a rudderless ship, he lacked the appetite for making prudent decisions with the aid of his officers. In short, he didn't relish the decision-making process. This is necessary for superior management, so the answer to the question should be "usually/often."

Some Fascinating Numbers

In my book *Inside Corporate America*, a study of 1,086 top and middle executives in the 115 headquarters, divisions, and subsidiaries of thirteen major corporations, I reported some fascinating data on decision-making preferences.

When asked to choose between "most," "less," and "least frequent," 57 percent of the top executives in my study said that they most frequently reach decisions in collaboration with their subordinates.

In contrast, among middle managers the figure dropped to 38 percent.

What These Numbers Show

These numbers show that the collaborative decision-making process is more prevalent among executives who have made it to the top of their corporations than among those who have been passed over or have yet to get there.

This is true somewhat because top executives know less about the technical aspects of their business than the middle managers who report to them. They're more dependent on the specific knowledge of their subordinates than their subordinates are on their own subordinates' knowledge.

But top executives are also more experienced and wiser. The almost 20 percent differential between the two levels on collaborating to reach decisions shows that those in the highest positions of authority know that autocratic styles are less effective.

Collaboration is the way to reach prudent decisions in today's complex corporations made up of knowledge workers. Yet making it work is difficult, and one must be ever a student of its processes to do so. My client wasn't and never did make it work. Today he's captain of a battered hull. All his good executives have jumped ship.

TAKE ACTION

1. Check your impulse to run to the closet when approaching decisions.
2. Actual final decisions themselves will always rest with you, but work to elicit the best options from your subordinates.

45

WHEN THE HEAT IS ON

Q: When you must oppose a
group decision, are you willing
to take the heat?

A: Usually/Often _____
Sometimes/Seldom _____

I ONCE SERVED on a search committee for a not-for-profit association of which I am a member. The board members asked me to participate because they thought my experience as a search consultant could be of benefit. This made sense to me, of course, and because I cared deeply about the organization's work, I agreed to sign on.

Our search was for a new president and CEO. The current one had just announced his retirement after a twenty-year tenure of distinction. Some wondered, I among them, whether we ever could find a suitable successor. The incumbent wore a big mantle gracefully.

All but one of fifteen members of the search committee were on other standing committees and therefore represented some constituency of this large association. Several had spent one or more terms on the rotating board of directors. One member was the sitting board chairman, a volunteer position. The chairman of the search committee itself was a former board chairman and a man whose dedication to the association had been proved over years—culminating in his willingness to take on this headache of a job.

I was the one nonrepresentative committee member. I was acquainted with my fellow members in name only, and had to content myself with knowing that my presence was due to (1) my being an association member, (2) my having been vocal on an issue at one public meeting, and (3) my expertise. "Not much of a power base," I thought.

Résumés, Dossiers, and Vitae

Our search took fifteen months. As a full committee, we met monthly for hours at a time. Subcommittees met in addition to the monthly meetings. Between meetings each of us pored over résumés, dossiers, and vitae of potential candidates for the job. The search was not confidential, and because it was known about throughout the trade and considered an attractive position, the network produced a flood of applicants and recommendations.

Eventually, six candidates emerged as most appropriate, with one clear front-runner among them. The sentiments of almost all the committee were with this man because he had a good track record and came strongly recommended by respected parties.

I didn't agree and kept quiet, as there were still too many candidates in the field and I was hopeful the lead candidate would stumble without any intervention from me. A lot can be told from the way a person writes up a dossier, and I felt that this man's reflected excessive vanity.

All six candidates were interviewed and the field was reduced to two: (1) the front-runner, who remained so but to my mind confirmed my suspicions, and (2) also, to my mind, a far superior candidate.

"No, I Don't Think So"

That's what I said to my stunned associates when the almost rhetorical question came up about the front-runner being the best person for the job. And let me tell you, I felt the heat!

Second meetings for both candidates were scheduled. References were conducted. The charm and charisma of the front-runner faded to an embarrassing self-centeredness, which the references confirmed, and the tortoise passed the hare.

The selected candidate is now in his fourth year as CEO. Although his predecessor was a person who many of us thought left shoes too big to fill, we are indeed gratified at having found the right man for this stage in our association's development. Dues are up. Membership is up. Programming is expanding. Spirit is up. Participation is up.

When I first voiced my view about the front-runner, I ruffled many feathers. After the second interviews, I made some allies. By the time the search was over, I had made some lifelong friends.

I'm glad I took the heat. The answer to the question, as you know well by now, should be "usually/often."

TAKE ACTION

1. When the time is right, and you've examined the evidence, take your stand and be willing to go against the grain. Those who don't thank you at first may thank you later.
2. Take comfort in knowing that the heat tempers your future judgment. You get smarter and more self-confident.

46

A GOAL
IN ITS TIME

Q: **Do you set goals before
their time?**

A: Usually/Often _____
Sometimes/Seldom _____

IT WAS ALMOST twenty years ago that I was reading an article in the then newly launched magazine *Psychology Today*. I'm able to place it in time because I read it on a Chicago commuter train during the year my wife and I—confirmed city dwellers—gave suburban living a whirl. (We lasted nine months. One night my wife met me at the 6:12 and announced, "It's Barrington or me!")

At any rate, one morning while bound for downtown Chicago, I got engrossed in this article written by Peter Drucker. Even then he had long been a management guru, and I gobbled up everything he wrote. I was especially fascinated with this article, however, because it was about managing one's career. Being a fledgling executive search consultant with Spencer Stuart & Associates—at the time the largest search firm in the world—I felt that it had obvious application to my work.

As always, Drucker laced this piece with ample wit and wisdom, but he made one exclamation that attached itself to my thoughts and has never let go. Pointing to himself, Drucker wrote, "Here I am, fifty-eight years old, and I don't know what I'm going to do when I grow up." Now nearing eighty, this Vienna-born genius hasn't changed. He'll go to his grave a child.

The Journey

The eloquence of Drucker's exclamation is to be grasped both in his realization that many of his goals have not yet been met and in his obvious joy over discovering that many have yet to be *set*. And he makes clear, though indirectly, how easy it is to make the mistake of setting goals before their time.

He knows very well that the answer to the question should be "sometimes/seldom."

There is a further lesson from Drucker's words. It is that he is referring to short-term and intermediate goals, not that central one that constitutes what could be called his life theme. Despite his overstatement, he *does* know what he will be when he grows up. He will be what he has always been: a man of great force through the exercise of his mind and pen.

What he is telling us is that he does not know how that theme will be played out in all its particulars, and that life and work are journeys in which the most critical and refreshing element is discovery.

The Rhythm

If our life themes are basically inviolable, as I believe they are, we ought to pay more attention to them in setting our goals. In other words, we need to put our own ear to our own ground. Executives are not good at this. Control, not discovery, is what they're after, and their outer actions often end up in dissonance with their inner selves.

A goal of being a community leader, for example, is laudable and might be absolutely right for you, but perhaps it should be undertaken in five or ten years rather than today. Something else should be given your energies now. A right goal set prematurely spins wheels, leads to frustration and failure, and lowers one's self-esteem.

Let life unfold as discovery, and it will suggest energizing goals compatible with the rhythm of your life theme. This is the secret of a Peter Drucker and others like him.

TAKE ACTION

1. Before setting any goals at all, focus inward until you find your central core. What is your life really all about? Does this goal really fit?
2. If left with a true goal, determine whether it's a goal for now or later. If it's for later, put it into storage.

47

CUTTING FOR
THE BALL

Q: **Do you determine what area
of your company would
benefit most from superior
performance by you?**

A: Usually/Often _____
Sometimes/Seldom _____

LET ME GIVE you the answer to the question right away. It should be "usually/often." Let me also point out right away that many of us are slow to catch on to this notion. To use an expression from football, we don't cut for the ball. We're like the receiver who doesn't dash at the right time to the place on the field where he knows the quarterback is going to throw the ball. I, for one, am an example of this, and would like to be personal in this chapter.

Early on I was trained as a sociologist. I taught that subject at the college level for three years. I also completed postgraduate studies at the Alfred Adler Institute in Chicago and qualified for membership in the American Group Psychotherapy Association.

Then I went into business at age twenty-seven. Armed with this knowledge of group behavior and having been a student of large-scale organizations and social movements, I joined an executive search firm. I formed my own firm four years later—specializing in search—and even was fortunate enough to write a popular book about my trade: *Confessions of a Corporate Headhunter*.

Search is a way a company seeks a solution to a business problem with primary emphasis on the individual. Undeniably, search often is imperative. But I must point out—and coming from me, this may puzzle you—it's abused and fails because it's often called upon when an organizational or team solution is needed.

Wrong Image

One night my wife and I were out to dinner with a client of mine and his spouse. The client, now retired, was one I admired, and we had worked together effectively for over a decade. Jointly we had completed numerous top-management searches. As a tough-minded vice president of human resources of a diversified corporation with multibillion-dollar sales, he took such searches seriously. So you know how pleased and flattered I was that he voted his belief in my competence with repeat work and the thousands of dollars in fees that he invested in me.

You can imagine my surprise, then, when his wife turned to me at one point in the conversation and said, "Allan, you seem to be embarrassed to be in the search business."

Well, she was dead wrong in her conclusion, but she had done me an enormous favor by picking up some vibes I was sending out. My offhand remarks about the abuses of search had led her to believe I wasn't committed to it.

Wrong Context

From that evening, I wheeled and regrouped. I saw from her remarks that if I was going to continue my professional growth I had to place my commitment to search in the right context. Right for my clients. Right for me. I could see that over the long haul, my whole business depended on it. I changed that context from being a searcher who does organizational consulting to an organizational consultant who does searches. I finally (fifteen years after entering business) had cut for the ball!

On a different course, in 1982 I published *The Cox Report on the American Corporation*, a corporate culture study that *Publishers Weekly* called "a survey-science *tour de force*." I followed that up with *The Making of the Achiever*, a book about the "team way" of succeeding in American business. Moreover, the organizational development and top-management team-building thrust that came upon corporations played directly to my strengths. In other words, I'd hit stride.

I still do searches, and they're as key as ever. We're still listed as one of the leading fifty search firms by *Executive Recruiter News*, the watchdog of the industry. But the searches are done sparingly and come out of client relationships where I'm more knowledgeable, so that I can offer advice on whether they're a likely solution.

I know all this sounds like a big brag, but I don't mean it that way. Rather, what bears emphasis is that although I came late to the game, I eventually discovered where superior performance by me would have the most impact, and it has made all the difference in what I have to contribute and the satisfaction I derive from my work.

And my most important point is this: *The same can be true for you.*

TAKE ACTION

1. Ask yourself whether anyone has been sending you valuable signals like those my client's wife sent me over dinner. If so, don't ignore them. They can change your life. Feedback is a gift!
2. Ask yourself whether you're where you function at your personal best. But keep in mind that for most of us, the "where" is an attitude. Nothing changed physically for me when I cut for the ball.

48

EXPECTATIONS OF PERFORMANCE —NOT CAREER— MAKE THE DIFFERENCE

Q: Do you follow up your flashes of insight with planning and hard work?

A: Usually/Often _____
Sometimes/Seldom _____

MY FAVORITE PART of *The Wall Street Journal* is the front page of Section 2. There, people and topics of interest to business executives are always treated in a fresh, succinct way.

The November 14, 1986, issue carried a feature on this page titled "More Executives Finding Changes in Traditional Corporate Ladder." The article indicated that massive restructuring and downsizing in corporate America, combined with the glut of baby boomers, has left many executives without the advancement opportunities they anticipated when joining the work force.

Back in the late 1960s when the American economy, despite the social upheaval taking place, was reaching a crest, and our corporate payrolls were bulging at the seams, I had a friend who got a big laugh out of a bunch of us sitting around a bar one night waiting for our commuter trains to arrive and take us to suburbia.

What he asked was, "Do you realize what trouble we'd be in if everybody did his job?"

Career Expectations

I have another friend, Professor Douglas Lamont of Northwestern's business school, who came at the same subject from the opposite end when he published a book in 1986 entitled *Forcing Our Hand*. It eloquently shows, among other things, how foreign competitors are compelling all American employees to do their jobs. And yes, we're in trouble.

Of course, my first friend's point was that if all of us did our jobs, we wouldn't need bloated payrolls, and a lot of people would be on the street. My second friend's point was that we simply can't afford unproductive people any longer, and that's why many are now on the street.

These persons casting about for other jobs have lower career expectations than they once did. But that's also true of those who are fortunate enough to have survived corporate purges.

Performance Expectations

There's something very good about all this, however. We have been forced to recognize that career *satisfaction* is possible only through living up to high performance expectations, not perfunctory career advancement. It is the former that is leading us to renewed competitiveness with our foreign neighbors. It is satisfying to put ourselves to a stern test and gather strength as we begin to sense that we can meet it. That is what skill building is all about.

Eric Hoffer noted that what is unique and worthwhile in us makes itself felt in flashes. We all have these flashes of insight and useful impulse, but it is the achiever bent on quality performance who follows them up with planning and hard work.

Such a flash occurred to a woman described in the piece in *The Wall Street Journal*. She realized that performance is what matters and that she would have to move sideways before she could move up. A research manager at a large electronics company, she "deduced that her employer—in the throes of changing its product mix—needed to beef up training and development. She volunteered for the job and was so successful she has become a vice president."

Be like this woman, who knows that the answer to the question should be "usually/often."

TAKE ACTION

1. See what is needed. Remember that performance is what really counts.
2. Be willing to tread unfamiliar turf to find where you can perform at your best and make the most significant contribution. Then give it all you've got.

49

SIGNING UP
OR SIGNING OUT

Q: **Do you view your actual work with your associates as the only part of yourself you owe to the team?**

A: Usually/Often _____
Sometimes/Seldom _____

RECENTLY I BEGAN a team-building assignment for a chief executive and the nine top executives who report to him.

This group and I met for three days at a conference center away from their headquarters. Our task was to start to forge a team out of a loose—and sometimes warring—aggregate of talented people.

My job as a consultant was to serve as a facilitator, and I did it. The meeting was judged a success by all participants, and the prevailing sentiment was that indeed this group had much more to gain by pulling together rather than apart.

This corporation was a brand-new client for me, and in the interviews I conducted among these ten executives in preparation for our three days together off-site, I was meeting all but one of them for the first time.

Right at the end of this session, after I had summarized for the group what values they had agreed on that would guide their behavior in becoming a team, one of the executives complimented me on how well I had come to know them so quickly. They all gave me a short burst of applause. Then, in a quick rejoinder, the CEO said, "Allan now knows all of us, but we don't know Allan."

An Invitation

This "fast take" by the CEO seemed lost in the collective goodwill of the applause sent my way, sort of like water spilled on sand. But I got the message, and to my delight, it struck me not as a criticism or barb, but as an invitation.

I was being asked in. If I was going to continue to work with these people in an effective way, I was going to have to sign up, and a given in all this was that the team would want to know what makes *me* tick. I would not be allowed to maintain a "hygienic distance."

Although the CEO's comment was an invitation, unknown to him I took it as a personal warning too. I did so because I tend to be aloof in some cases, and strangely silent in others, where I'm ever the observer and stingy in giving of myself. This can make people feel judged and, to say the least, ill at ease.

Being Accessible

The answer to the question should be "sometimes/seldom." If you find that criticism is often laid at your doorstep for not being accessible physically or emotionally to the people you work with, you can be sure that much vital information will pass by your house. You simply won't know what's going on in the minds of your peers, and your subordinates will tell you merely what you want to hear.

More important, by isolating yourself behind closed doors or a personal shield, you're keeping what's inside from coming out. That is, what's unique and worthwhile in you is seldom seen, used, or appreciated.

As I began this assignment it would be critical for me to follow my own advice.

TAKE ACTION

1. Loosen up. If all your blemishes are covered by your clothing, disrobe a little!
2. Work, work, work is a formula for failure. Join the team. Doing less is doing more.

50

BEYOND "ME TOO" STRENGTHS

Q: When taking initiative, are you willing to move out of your comfort zone?

A: Usually/Often _____
Sometimes/Seldom _____

In a workshop with a group of general-management executives with Holiday Inns not long ago, I looked at a woman in the group and said: "Let's forget about business for a minute. Jewell, suppose your college roommate calls you up, tells you she's getting married, and then says she wants you to sing at her wedding.

"Instantaneously you go into shock, your heart starts pounding, and you barely can speak. Your mind races and indulges in all kinds of imagined catastrophes.

"You recover enough to remember that it's awfully nice to be asked. After all, you do have a nice voice. But all you ever did was sing with your college a cappella choir and perform all right on a couple of short solos. Yet even that threw you into a fright, and that was ten years ago!

"You stammer that you just can't do it, how flattering it is of your old friend to want you to do it, but that, no, you just *can't*!

"However, the bride-to-be has known you for a long time and well. She says, 'Oh, come on, Jewell, you have a beautiful voice, and it would really mean a lot to me.'

"That does it. You relent, agree to do it, get shivers every time you think about it, rehearse like hell, do it, excel, and feel like a million dollars."

Now, of course, I wouldn't have "picked on" Jewell with this example if I hadn't come to know her earlier in the workshop. I think a lot of her and know her associates do too. She responded, in fact, by saying a parallel situation had occurred to her over the past weekend. She had always had the urge to try deep sea diving but was, at the same time, afraid to. She bit her lip and agreed to do it off the Florida coast. It was as exhilarating as she expected it to be and she feels "stronger and more self-confident" in all aspects of her life because of her decision to take the fearful plunge.

Finding Our Unique Strengths

The answer to the question should be "usually/often." It's imperative that we be willing to move out of our comfort zones.

What I mean by this is that we set apart our unique strengths from our commodity strengths and act on them.

Our commodity strengths are the price of admission to the game. They are, for the most part, our professional credentials. They include our education, experience, and training. But they are "me too" strengths. So, you're an accountant with a CPA? So what? So, you're a Stanford MBA? So are three alcoholics I know. So, you're a mechanical engineer from Purdue? So are 50,000 others.

Jewell has the credentials to do her job. She's a professional manager and a good one. But in the hypothetical case I threw at her as an example for the whole group, her unique strength was the rare ability to deliver an oral message artistically and persuasively.

Facing Down Fear

To find our unique strengths, we have to exhume them. They're buried. We've ignored them, discarded them. We've done that because they frightened us somehow. To act on them is to take a risk. Jewell didn't know whether she was going to win enthusiastic praise or embarrassed silence.

To act on a unique strength is to face down a fear. It is to acknowledge that pebble in your shoe but keep walking. It is to realize that something you care about down deep and want to express somehow also scares you to death.

Jacques Maritain, the late French philosopher and theologian, wrote: "The man of courage flees forward."

TAKE ACTION

1. Want to be a truly value-added executive? Start by naming a task that scares you and also appeals to you.
2. Consent with yourself and others to take it on. Consent *now*.

51

MAKING THE
NOW DECISION

Q: **Do you ask yourself what the most important decision is that you should make *now*?**

A: Usually/Often _____
    Sometimes/Seldom _____

How common it is to clutter our work lives and thoughts with decisions we can't or shouldn't make. We often toss the plans, events, hopes, fears, joys, sorrows, losses, victories, boos, applause, dreads, and delights of past, present, and future into some sort of on-the-job grab bag. Then we take this odd, lumpy assortment of cares by its neck and stash it—not right on top of our desks, where it would be far too obstructive—but over in one of the far corners of our office. There it's out of the way, but always plainly in view and readily accessible.

That's My Bag!

That's what you think as you walk into your work space each morning and glance at it periodically throughout the day. Each little bulge in the bag, as well as each invisible article inside, represents a factor in some decision to be made. Every day the bag gets bigger because you cram another article or two into it. Now it is stuffed beyond its capacity and about to burst at the seams.

The question is what to take out. Each article has an importance all its own. Taking any one out will relieve some of the pressure on the bag, at least temporarily, but the trouble is that all the items seem to deserve your attention right now.

Get Rid of the Bag!

Get rid of it because it is a lumpy, slouching bag of cares with no spine. It is a chaotic mass that does not allow for orderly selection based on current need. It takes on a life of its own and obscures what decisions take priority today. The answer to the question should be "usually/often."

It is always tempting to fret over past failures or savor anticipated triumphs rather than simply face up to what decisions need to be made *now*. When you hear footsteps from the past or dream of accolades that may turn out to elude you, current affairs tend to get neglected and you needlessly (and perhaps harmfully) compromise your present.

The decision is the discipline. It is the decision that must be served. And decisions must be made about decisions, the main one being whether or not a decision is one for now or one for later. If it's for later, put it aside. In so doing you'll know what should be stored and labeled for use in making that decision at that future time.

In deciding what needs to be decided now, you'll eliminate the clutter in your life. You'll build most prudently on your past successes and stand the best chance of having people forget your failures. Likewise, you'll enhance your future by showing all onlookers not only that you know how to do things right, but that you do the right things.

TAKE ACTION

1. Declare yourself independent from worries about all the decisions that you have to make in the next three to six months. Make good on this declaration by giving all your resources and attention to the decision that you have to make now.

2. Perhaps you don't have to make a decision now. Enjoy the leisure! And by all means, do not make the mistake of trying to make a decision in the interim that can be made later. Don't just do something, stand there!

52

STEPPING
INTO THE NOW

Q: Do you postpone decisions
that should be made now?

A: Usually/Often _____
Sometimes/Seldom _____

IN THE LAST chapter I wrote about the importance of asking yourself what the most critical decision is that you should make now. In this one I'm writing about the same subject, but with a different shading. Whereas proper thought and analysis are necessary to *identify* key decisions to be made at present, courage needs to be combined with judgment in order to *act* on what you conclude.

The Hesitating Attitude

Alfred Adler maintained that for people truly to thrive at living, they have to overcome the hesitating attitude that is so characteristic of many of us.

"He who hesitates is lost," goes an old saying. Certainly, as discussed in Chapter 39, there are times when hesitating is the only prudent course. But still, the lesson from the old proverb is obvious: People who face decisions that can lead to distinctive outcomes only if they are made now—but who postpone them— are cutting themselves out of the action.

For this reason, the answer to the question should be "sometimes/seldom."

The purpose of postponement in most cases is also obvious: the avoidance of getting stuck with a high-stakes decision that turns out to be wrong. By pushing a decision into the future, we fool ourselves into thinking that better or more information will be forthcoming; that will increase the odds of making a wiser decision on the matter down the road. So we hope.

We also sense, but don't acknowledge fully, that making the decision now is only the first of many acts in a chain that can lead to desired results. Assuring the success of that decision is the hard part—and quite forbidding. If we postpone the immediate decision, we also sidestep all the complicated choices that will arise from it. This is a *not*-so-obvious reason to delay the first decision.

The Gap Between Now and Then

A novel, captivating idea relevant to this subject comes from another psychiatrist—this time Frederick Perls—a pioneer of Gestalt psychotherapy. Perls defined anxiety as the gap between the "now" and the "then." He said that whenever we're put on the spot and called on to perform at anything in any way, that gap in time between knowing we have to perform and the actual time of our performance is filled with discomfort at wondering whether we will get flowers or rotten tomatoes.

When the time for performance arrives and we step into the "now," said Perls, anxiety disappears to the degree that we bring all our resources to bear on our performance.

The lesson for us in this case is that by postponing decisions—an attempt at reducing anxiety—we actually increase and prolong it. In so doing we divert ourselves from total, committed effort to do what we should be doing now.

TAKE ACTION

1. Write down three decisions you think you should make now, but are hesitant to make. Place a check mark next to the one that calls out to you—that "wants doing" the most.
2. Acknowledge that the decision itself is only Step 1. Draft a detailed plan for what initiatives you must invest in for desired results, and step into the now.

53

A LESSON
FROM MAMA

Q: **Do you second-guess your decisions?**

A: Usually/Often _____
Sometimes/Seldom _____

In his semiautobiographical latest novel, *Inside, Outside*, Herman Wouk gives the reader a quick take on a slice of his and his sister's life growing up in Apartment 5A in a tenement house in the southeast Bronx.

He tells one of those delightful "Jewish mother" stories, in this case, about his own—"the big *yoxenta*" (Yiddish for a woman of breeding). This particular story offers a riveting lesson on decisiveness.

> How did mama cope with the hazard of small children loose in a fifth floor flat? Keeping the windows shut was no answer. Mama believed in fresh air, and anyway in the summertime we would have choked. No, what mama did when we moved in was to take Lee and then myself by the ankles, hold us one by one outside a window head-down, and let us scream and wriggle in terror for a good while at the sight of the drop to the concrete yard five stories below. That did it.

Make It Fast

Mrs. Goodkind, the storyteller's mother, didn't hack around. She reached a conclusion about what was required on her part to get desired results and she acted. It worked. End of story.

Twelve years ago, a friend of mine was executive vice president and a director of a company that sold $6 billion worth of consumer packaged goods every year. He went to his doctor for an annual physical, and was promptly sent to one of the leading cardiologists in his city. The cardiologist recommended coronary bypass surgery. Within a week the surgery was done, and my friend has lived a completely normal life ever since. Moreover, he started a business of his own when he retired eight years later.

At the time, my friend told me that he went ahead with the surgery immediately because he knew it was the right thing to do, and he didn't want to give himself the chance to get frightened by stewing over it.

If this kind of decision making can work so well in life-threatening situations, imagine how much sense it would make on our jobs.

Don't Look Back

Both the examples I've given involved circumstances where the information needed to make a decision was produced quickly.

That's not always the case, as we well know. Long, arduous fact-gathering missions, information-generating projects, and alternative-developing debates must often be entered into before we fully understand the courses of action available to us, along with their probable consequences.

So my point, first of all, is not merely to decide quickly, but to decide quickly once you have the necessary information.

Second, after you've made your decision, don't look back. Folkwise baseball great Satchell Page said, "Don't look back; somethin' might be gainin' on you." He again shows that the element of fear may enter, threatening one's performance.

In a race, the lead runner not only slows himself down by looking back, but breaks concentration and risks discouragement by seeing a competitor make gains. But by looking forward, the smart runner keeps eyes focused on the finish line, marshalls his full resources, and is more likely to assure victory as the final result.

This lets us know that the answer to the question should be "sometimes/seldom."

TAKE ACTION

1. Don't stew and let yourself get afraid. Be like my friend. If you know what you need to do, just do it. Put it behind you and keep it there.
2. Having done it, take a moment to pat yourself on the back for your resolve. Such decisiveness is rare.

54

LISTENING TO YOUR STOMACH

Q: **Does hindsight show your decisions to have been right ones?**

A: Usually/Often _____
Sometimes/Seldom _____

Earlier this week , I was leafing through a back issue of *New Management*. That's the refreshing quarterly magazine from the Graduate School of Business of The University of Southern California.

In so doing, I ended up rereading an essay by Ray Bradbury entitled "Management From Within." I had enjoyed this piece and found it thought-provoking the first time—over two years ago—but on this occasion it jelled even more for me because it fit so nicely with the subject of this chapter: intuition.

Bradbury writes:

> . . . on certain days, emulate Darwin.
> What did he do? He strolled out to stand in the middle of fields waiting for a bird to land on his shoulder, watching for the foxes to come home at dawn, listening to the sounds of the world and knowing delight as well as discovery.

Intuition and Caring

I have a favorite statement that I always make to executives when I'm asked to address them on the subject of their individual development. It goes like this: "You can't be good at your work if you don't care, and you can't care if you're not authentic."

Intuition and caring are partners in enterprise. If we pay attention to it, intuition tells us whatever it is we care about down deep; what we care about we make sure gets our utmost effort. The rub for many of us, though, is that with our bluster-filled lives, we often don't know what we care about.

It is a truism in business that for a project to be fruitful it has to have an objective. Yet my experience is that most executives approach their work not with an objective in mind, but an *ought*. A real objective is a *want*, not an ought; it's something you care about. Ya gotta wanna!

When I conduct an executive development workshop for a company's management team, I'll often open the session by asking the participants, one by one, what they want from it. I can tell from the facial expressions of some in the group that the question causes panic. They don't know what they want. And since they don't, they sure won't get it. Unless things change, this will be one more in a series of rudderless days.

Intuition and Hindsight

Intuition is shutting down the whirlwind and listening to your stomach. The late Frederick Perls used to say that to grasp life you have to "lose your mind and come to your senses." Selectively applied, that's great advice.

Having now spent over twenty years in the world of executive search and executive development, having interviewed thousands of executives, I can tell you that a well-worn theme of lament throughout these encounters is, "If I'd only listened to my gut on that one, it would have turned out right."

The intuitive executive is the one who can answer the question "usually/often."

TAKE ACTION

1.   Heed Ray Bradbury's concluding admonition: "Tomorrow, go stand in a field somewhere. You might just meet yourself, coming home, at noon, or as the sun sets, and your heart will know delight."
2.   Realize that the "field" is wherever you choose to make it.

55

BEING
A THOUGHTFUL
PRAGMATIST

Q: Do you maintain an animated,
inquiring, processing mind?

A: Usually/Often _____
Sometimes/Seldom _____

I HAVE JUST returned from a stimulating conference where about thirty of us spent three days with an extraordinary man. His name is Elliott Jaques. The conference was sponsored by the nifty, not-for-profit Center for Creative Leadership of Greensboro, North Carolina.

Jaques is an internationally respected scholar, researcher, writer, and thinker on organization and management. My role was panelist offering my views on the implications, applications, and shortcomings of his ideas to the assembled Center staff and assorted corporate executives. My charge was to do so from the standpoint of "what it takes to be a successful executive."

Jaques holds a Ph.D. in social relations from Harvard and an M.D. from Johns Hopkins. Clearly he's in a different league from most of us when it comes to intellectual pursuits. Yet such credentials pale to anyone who comes into contact with his writings and face-to-face presentations. His ability to generate ideas is awesome.

This man who currently is conducting a long-range comprehensive organizational consulting assignment with the U.S. Army is also the person who coined the term "mid-life crisis." For twenty-five years he maintained a thriving practice as a psychoanalyst in England. In addition, he is the author of thirteen books.

After the first full day of listening to his presentation, all of us were bordering on information overload. The executive sitting next to me, knowing of my formidable task as critic the next morning, said, "I'd be scared stiff if I had to do what you're going to do."

Inspired, Not Intimidated

Actually, I wasn't intimidated, not because Jaques's mastery wasn't everything I expected, but because he's someone who *welcomes information from every source*—even me. Moreover, although he is on another plane altogether, he was an inspiring reminder that if we in business could temper our bias for motion with more effort given to reflection, we'd make fewer poor decisions and eliminate more false starts.

The Need Not to Know

A couple of years ago, I was speaking to the one hundred top executives of a multinational forest-products company, based on the West Coast. These executives were gathered from around the world for their annual management meeting. I was humming right along, my points being well received, when I made a statement and felt the room turn to stone.

I was describing chief executives who have a phobic reaction to attitude or "climate" surveys in their companies. "Imagine," I said, "a CEO who doesn't want to know what's on the minds of his people! Such an executive has a need not to know."

I realized my mistake immediately. As soon as I uttered those words, the CEO, sitting in the front row, dropped his head. And just like that, the rest of the executives went down with their slumping boss. Later, I had confirmed for me that this CEO hates surveys.

A good speaker knows his audience, but I'm only mildly repentant at not knowing mine in this case. I'm not terribly sorry I said what I believe. Whereas Elliott Jaques is a lofty model of how fruitful inquiry can lead to extraordinary solutions, this CEO offered a lesson on how a closed mind shuts options down. Both examples show that the answer to the question should be "usually/often."

TAKE ACTION

1. Realize that being reflective doesn't make you indecisive or lacking in initiative.
2. Alert your mind. Processing information from unconventional quarters will generate unconventional alternatives. This will make you a thoughtful pragmatist.

56

LOOKING GOOD, BEING GOOD

Q: Do you spend your time and effort looking good rather than being good?

A: Usually/Often _____
Sometimes/Seldom _____

THERE ARE FAR too many people who face their work with the idea that they would rather look good than be good. They are the ones who always are seeking shortcuts and inside tips for getting a leg up the corporate ladder. They assume that all they need to reach the career summit is to avail themselves of a few secrets of success.

Looking Good

Probably the group most symbolic of this afflicted way of thinking are the throng that have swallowed the dress-for-success formula to satisfy their career appetites. I say symbolic because this fad just happens to be a current example of how some strivers will count on image rather than substance for arriving where they hope to.

To be sure, I have no quarrel with dressing the part. I myself take pains to dress as well as I know how, and advise all executives not to disqualify themselves from advancement for reasons of poor grooming, soup-stained ties, garish suits, dresses that look like they've been slept in, or unshined shoes with run-down heels. Actually, a recent Hart Schaffner & Marx ad captures my sentiments exactly: "The right suit might not grant entree to the boardroom. But the wrong suit may very well keep you out."

The ad slogan wisely conveys the message that dressing the part is merely supportive. It's quality performance that rivets the attention of others at center stage. Naturally, then, the answer to the question should be "sometimes/seldom."

Being Good

Another credential that not so long ago was assumed to have magical properties was the vaunted MBA degree. Moreover, if one could be obtained from a prestigious business school, all the better. Thousands of young, eager students expended great effort working hard for high grades to qualify themselves for these institutions.

Unfortunately, many of these young people in possession of the golden ticket soon discovered that their corporations placed higher value on other executives who offered something more than they did. A bit too full of themselves, they were easily disillusioned. This was partly because the American economy had come up against formidable foreign competition.

That "something more" that the other executives offered was commitment to performance and substance rather than rhetoric and image. They labored at being good at their tasks, rather than posturing and talking a good game.

Today, ironically, the MBA is making a low-key, credible comeback. Well, it should. There never was anything wrong with adding to one's education. As all good executives know, that's a lifelong undertaking. The problem was simply too many graduates believing that they already had learned it all, and that the climb to the top of their companies was a short, quick one.

TAKE ACTION

1. Make sure you're not working overtime at keeping up appearances as a substitute for sheer nitty-gritty performance. One way to start is by taking initiative on a nasty project that your company wants done, but that your associates are avoiding. Curry favor with your boss this way rather than trying to charm him to death and dazzle him with your wardrobe.

2. An MBA is not essential for reaching the pinnacle of success in the executive suite. But if you choose to go for one, vow that you're doing so to increase your knowledge, not to win a medal to pin on your chest and strut your stuff.

57

COMBATTING THE NEED NOT TO KNOW

Q: Are you good at finding holes in your corporation that need filling?

A: Usually/Often _____
Sometimes/Seldom _____

EARLY IN PRESIDENT Reagan's first term, late Commerce Secretary Malcolm Baldrige was heard to say that many top business executives are "fat, dumb, and happy." It's hardly surprising that his comment received wide press coverage.

Formidably Incurious

Actually, top executives are anything but dumb, and I'm sure Secretary Baldrige would agree. Every compilation of statistics I've seen on IQ has shown top executives to rank extremely high in this respect.

One study I saw a few years ago from Science Research Associates, an IBM testing subsidiary, rated them and medical doctors as the brightest of all professional groups. But I believe Secretary Baldrige had a point if what he meant is that many top executives are content to feed a frame of mind best described as "business as usual." Certainly, the fads that come and go—including what standards should suffice for measuring corporate performance—show that we are more at home with novelty than real innovation.

For my part, I am continually amazed at the number of chief executives unwilling to survey their people to learn what's on their minds. I know, I know . . . I've heard the argument for their position: "To survey our employees just creates expectations on which we can't deliver."

Baloney! Change the "can't" to "won't" and you've got the picture. Business as usual. I call it the need not to know. You read about one example of this in Chapter 55.

The Inquiring Disposition

What's required in the executive suite as much as anything else is the discovery of *what's missing*. This is what I mean by "holes." What isn't there that ought to be? Addressing this issue is critical and makes the better answer to the question "usually/often."

Many executives see and deal only with what's there, whereas the executives most valuable to their corporations are the ones who see what isn't there. One of the cutest examples of this from the annals of consumer marketing was the researcher who discovered the hole in his company's marketing of cake mix. What was missing was the consumer's input into the baking process. This discovery led the company to take the powdered egg out of the mix that was bought off the supermarket shelf. When the consumer added the egg, this was found to provide a more rewarding baking experience. Sales soared.

Within a given company, perhaps a sales training department is needed where none exists. Or perhaps a sales training department that exists can be eliminated because the real hole is one-to-one sales training in the field.

Perhaps the new structure of office of the chairman has called attention to the hole in the corporation's ability to make clear-cut decisions and communicate them from the top. This is the structure adopted by several companies where two or three executives at the very top, such as chairman, vice chairman, and president, consider and announce their decisions as a body of one. This kind of curiosity is what lets management know where its company is headed and what its options are.

TAKE ACTION

1. Take inventory of your frame of mind to determine whether you're "fat, dumb, and happy."
2. Give vent to your natural curiosity. Be assured that commitment to the discipline of discovery is not frivolous. The survival of your company depends on it.

58

GOT HOLES
IN THE KNEES OF
YOUR JEANS?

Q: **Are you willing to admit to holes in your confidence that need filling?**

A: Usually/Often _____
    Sometimes/Seldom _____

LINCOLN DUNCAN IS the teenage subject of a Paul Simon song about leaving home. "Home" was poverty-wracked with a father who was a fisherman and a mother who was the "fisherman's friend." Heading down the turnpike from the Maritimes to New England, he declares to himself: "Holes in my confidence/Holes in the knees of my jeans."

Holes in My Confidence

Last week, I had the glorious confirmation of having filled a hole in my confidence. Here's what took place: I went on a sales call and made the sale!

Sound simple? It isn't. I'd been asked by the vice president of human resources of a well-known industrial-chemicals corporation to meet with him and the chief executive to explore the possibility of doing a search for president of the company's largest division.

The executive search firm I manage is a small one, and the competition I faced for this high-level assignment was made up—as it almost always is—of the megafirms. These are the ones with offices scattered around the world, associates numbering as high as 250, with a "computerized research network," they all like to say, "that's unrivaled in the business."

For some time, the hole in my confidence was selling. By that, I mean being persuasive with strangers from whom I was going to collect sizable fees. Now, I enjoy a decent reputation in my field, so I've always had my share and lived well enough. But there often were times I didn't get business I wanted because I thought when I met with prospective clients that my reputation would sell itself.

Whereas many people speak when they should listen, I often sat quietly when I should have spoken. These days, however, I tell my story and seldom lose the business that I truly want to get.

Holes in My Jeans

Most of us start out just like Lincoln Duncan. But we go to school, go to work, learn the ropes, and develop our poise. We round ourselves out, hang out our shingle, figuratively speaking, and people know how they can count on us.

But the years go by, and in the climbing and striving, we lose touch with a thing or two that we once were really good at. A hole opens up and we're not as assertive and caring as we were. We go flat, and you know where it shows up? In our jeans.

Oh, not the literal jeans, of course. But perhaps our grooming in some other way. Or our posture; the onset of slouch may lay bare our dampened spirit; we may walk ploddingly rather than with the old bounce in our step. And faces . . . my god, our faces! As Abraham Lincoln remarked, "Every man over forty is responsible for his face."

So here I am at the "late" age of forty-nine, tickled at having reestablished contact with something I'd disowned. What about you? Won't you agree that the answer to the question should be "usually/often?"

TAKE ACTION

1. Close the door and put your feet up and ponder what's happening in your life. Isn't something missing that was there?
2. Reclaim it in whole or part by moving out of your comfort zone. There's something important that needs doing by you in your company, but you have to chip off the barnacles before you can do it.

59

AN EMPOWERED SELF, EMPOWERING OTHERS

Q: **Are you good at convincing your associates that a hole in your company can be filled?**

A: Usually/Often _____
     Sometimes/Seldom _____

GARY DILLON IS the tall, lanky CEO of Household Manufacturing, Inc. In turn, Household Manufacturing is the almost $1-billion-volume subsidiary of Household International. This company, known most readily for its financial services arm that we see in the form of the ubiquitous neighborhood loan office under the red letters HFC.

Household International also owned National Car Rental until early 1987, when it was sold. In addition, Household Merchandising, a $3-billion-volume corporation, was spun off by the parent company in a leveraged buyout to its management about two years earlier.

For all of 1988, the two businesses that remain under the Household International umbrella—financial services and manufacturing—will earn more profit than the four businesses did when they were combined. More profit on half the volume!

Financial services always has been a strong business, and its profits have continued to grow. On the other hand, manufacturing was not a healthy business, but it is now, and its profits are beginning to soar. The reason? The impact of Gary Dillon.

An Empowered Self

Nine years ago I sat in a room of the Radisson South Hotel in Minneapolis with Gary Dillon. I had interviewed him and liked what I saw. He had enjoyed a steady climb up the ladder at Pillsbury Corporation, and I knew immediately that Pillsbury would hate to lose him.

He'd spent eighteen years with Pillsbury, rising through plant operations. He and his family moved repeatedly, but had returned to Minneapolis a few years before our meeting when he became director of operations at headquarters. Then, two years later, his boss called him in and startlingly told him that Pillsbury wanted him to become general sales manager of the grocery products division. This man, who never had sold any-thing in a formal way, was being asked to take over the entire sales force of Pillsbury's flagship division. Do you realize how exceptional a situation this is? No one would be asked to make this long a leap were it not for his possession of out-standing leadership abilities. He accepted the position and ex-celled at it.

I was talking with Gary Dillon because I'd been retained by Household to recruit a possible successor to the CEO of its manufacturing business. In a couple of years, this CEO would retire, and Household president Don Clark told me that the company had no one to replace him.

This was one big *people* hole in the organization and a person like Dillon was needed. I found him, but he filled it. That's one kind of hole.

Empowering Others

I learned from studying Household's manufacturing business that it had many other holes as well. These were *performance* holes, and it soon became clear that Gary would build a team and convince and empower its members to fill them, one by one. The story is too long to tell here, but suffice it to say that the CEO did retire, Gary did take over, and he built a struggling $200 million business into a robust one over five times its size. Its best days lie ahead. Gary knows very well that the answer to the question should be "usually/often."

Nothing he's done is exotic; none of it requires me to fill the page with citations of sophisticated management techniques. But what he's done is rare; namely, he has insisted that his peo-ple stretch. He has forced on them a discipline for professional and personal growth. He's made them believe in themselves. That belief is captured in a theme he announced at a recent Household management conference: "We have found the edge and it is us."

TAKE ACTION

1. Find the edge and learn it's *you*! Do you remember my Opening Word to this book? Remember my question? "What quality design features are you continuing to build into your own performance profile?"
2. Then see what performance holes exist in your company that you can convince others to join you in filling.

60

REORDERING YOUR WORK BASKET

Q: **Do your goals turn out to be wishful thinking?**

A: Usually/Often _____
Sometimes/Seldom _____

IN CHAPTER 55, I wrote about being a panelist at a three-day conference sponsored by the Center for Creative Leadership. My job was to react to the ideas presented there by the central resource person, Elliott Jaques.

Jaques, you may recall my saying, is on another plane from most of us, and his fertile mind generates worthy ideas minute by minute.

My opening remarks to the conference—built around my appointed theme of what it takes to be a successful executive— were in praise of a two-part notion of his that is seemingly simple, yet incredibly powerful. That notion is:

1. "If a task doesn't have a maximum target completion time, it doesn't exist."
2. "In multiple tasks, it's always the longest task that determines your time span and sets your work basket."

By way of knitting these two parts together, Jaques would say that the most important question a subordinate should ask, whether of his boss or himself, is "When?" When is the job to be done? Without a set completion time a task becomes a phantom, regardless of whether it is assigned by one's boss or self-assigned.

Real Goals

Stop and think for a moment only about Jaques's first point. Think about how many goals get wafted about the executive suite. They fall more into the category of shibboleths or admonitions. They just sort of hang in the air as a comforting vapor of familiar rhetoric, vague good intentions that get coupled with words such as "should," "ought," and "try."

Here are some examples. "One of these days, we should do something about plant safety." "We ought to spend more money on executive development." "We've got to try to get our message across to the community." No deadline, no gathering of resources, no results. Just words.

This leads me to conclude, however, that the question "When?" is not enough. We need also to ask, "Oh, really?" I say this because a goal's being stated doesn't automatically mean that it's a real goal, even if it's marked by a completion date. Such goals, whether assigned by bosses or ourselves, can also be merely rhetorical or wishful thinking.

Choosing the right *when*'s and making sure each goal is real will allow you to answer the question "sometimes/seldom."

Long-Range Goals

The second part of Jaques's notion is especially intriguing. On our jobs, we can't allow ourselves to be absorbed by a single task. Rather, we have to juggle many initiatives, and they sometimes have competing priorities.

The implications of what Jaques is saying is that a real goal, set long term (let's say from three to twenty years), forges clear priorities and reduces disorganization in our current work life. That long-range goal—if it is real, legitimate, and *right for you*—is what gives added meaning to current time and space. The *then* desired outcome sets the tone, pace, quality, and appropriateness of your *now* efforts. Another way of saying this is that without a long-range goal, we drown ourselves in trivia and wishes.

Were he to know of your reading this, he might warn, as he did a few times at the conference, "Ignore this at your peril!"

TAKE ACTION

1. A long-range goal makes you focus on what's currently important. Think about what you truly want accomplished in three or more years.
2. Keep in mind that you will serve your organization and yourself best by making sure that your various initiatives and intermediate goals are in support of this central critical goal.

61

YA GOTTA BELIEVE!

Q: **Do your associates see you as a person who doesn't give up easily?**

A: Usually/Often _____
Sometimes/Seldom _____

W E TEND TO pull for the underdog. When we stop to think about it, though, there's an element of detachment in such support. If our favorite team or athlete is expected to win some contest, we hope the odds are well founded and that our team will trounce its opponent, no matter how much the underdog.

Belief in Something

One thing is certain about executives who don't give up easily. They aren't detached. They believe in what they're doing. They have to because they repeatedly encounter opponents who, for all kinds of reasons, want to shoot them down. Their opponents aren't detached either.

It's easy being a benign bystander pulling for someone in our company who is facing an uphill battle to get an idea accepted, or a project funded. That's so because we're not fully involved. Moreover, we enjoy hearing stories of victorious underdogs. We shake our heads in admiration, sensing that it may have been tough going, but escaping the gut-wrenching because we weren't part of the events. What's more, the story describing what occurred over months or years is told in a matter of minutes, thereby availing us of the happy ending in short order. No pain.

Are you detached about something in your company in which you're supposed to be invested? If so, your associates already know it and you're not going to be able to drum up support for it. You have to either declare yourself separated from it or find something in it you believe in and hunker down for the long pull.

Taking the Heat

Your associates will put you to the test. Returning to the sports analogy, it's painless to root for the underdog when neither team is your favorite. Then, if the underdog loses, you can walk away from the contest glibly offering compliments of noble effort and so on. But for the underdog's die-hard fans, losing *hurts*. Being involved has its risks!

For this reason, your associates aren't automatically going to take you at your word when you announce your intentions on a risky project and seek their support. They will examine your record for fortitude and take your measure in a dozen other ways before signing up. It's clear, then, that the answer to the question should be "usually/often."

Taking the heat means to deal resourcefully with criticism and self-doubts that spring from it. It is to grasp that just because someone has something bad to say about what you're doing, that person isn't necessarily right, certainly not completely. We learn from criticism, but there are times, too, when we should ignore it, not because it lacks merit, but so we won't be dissuaded from our main goal—the one we insist on reaching, no matter how haltingly.

TAKE ACTION

1. Ya gotta believe! Sort out the projects you face, and note those you care about most deeply. You simply won't do all you "ought to do," no matter how noble your intentions, or how deep your devotion to your boss's expectations. Get such required work out of the way as fast and conscientiously as you can, or hand it over to a promising subordinate. Then concentrate on what you believe in. Keep in mind, too, that your boss's interests and yours are not as incompatible as often appears. I'll have more to say about that in Chapter 93.
2. Cultivate a self-image in which you see yourself as a prevailer. That is, be the kind of person who refuses to wince under the sting of criticism. Give yourself time to see if you're mistaken. Ignore hair-trigger opinions.

62

NO PAIN, NO GAIN

Q: **Do you maintain a sturdy threshold for emotional pain?**

A: Usually/Often _____
Sometimes/Seldom _____

THE PROFESSOR ADDRESSED the sixty premed college juniors in the first class of the course in organic chemistry. He told them to look around the room at their fellow students. He then said that only one-fourth of them would get an A or B, and the rest should forget about applying to medical school. Without the coveted A or B in this critical course, they never would be admitted.

Maintaining the Threshold

Students in virtually every field come to that one course or professor who lets them know if they can't make it here, they're probably not going to make it at all. They had better find something else.

Such cut-the-mustard thresholds, while critical in school, are even more so in adult lives and careers. We arrive at junctures where we're forced to discover whether we're willing to pay the price to excel at what we do or want to do.

In "The Making of the Achiever" workshop I conduct in corporations, I strive to make this clear. But I find that when the company bringing me in has assembled a younger group of executives for the workshop, such as their "high-potential, marked-for-stardom comers," this point is harder to get across.

Lately I've adopted the style of the chemistry professor. I tell them that by age forty-five—the point at which most executives have been promoted into top management, if they're going to be—three-fourths of them won't have accomplished enough to make the cut and be top-flight achievers.

Emotional Pain

Executives who become high achievers, including those who for some reasons aren't selected for high-potential groups when they first begin their careers, are the ones who realize early on that they will have to withstand fierce assaults on their emotions.

Executives in their late twenties and early thirties, many of them labeled fast-trackers, are inclined to look to the "hard stuff" (facts, formulas, inside information) to get and stay ahead. Those who persist in doing so learn too late, if at all, that it is the "soft stuff" (wisdom born of literal suffering) that leads to distinction in one's work (and all of life, for that matter).

Now by suffering I mean only that without agony there can be no ecstasy. Speaking of emotional pain, well-known author Rabbi Harold Kushner says it best: "Don't be afraid of pain; it is nature's way of telling you that you're alive."

One bright young executive in a recent workshop was quite annoyed with my stressing tenacity as a poignant example of agony. She pointedly told me that many people hang on to something too long when they should just admit it isn't working out and never will, and let it go.

She's absolutely right, of course. But this is so in the minority of cases. Far more often, we fail at an undertaking simply because we won't bear the pain and discouragement of sticking with it. This means the answer to the question should be "usually/often."

TAKE ACTION

1. Prepare yourself mentally for hard knocks. Sometimes fate favors us on the road to achievement, but most often we reach our goals only after numerous failures and occasional bouts of self-doubt. Don't compound your difficulties by expecting otherwise.

2. Stop and celebrate your periodic accomplishments as you move along. The aftertaste of victory will fuel your appetite the next time you face tough going.

63

AVOIDING BURNOUT

Q: **Do you fail to learn and grow from your losses?**

A: Usually/Often _____
Sometimes/Seldom _____

I'M ALMOST HALFWAY through a terrific mystery novel. It's entitled *When the Bough Breaks* and written by Jonathan Kellerman.

The main character in the book is Dr. Alex Delaware, a supremely gifted and committed child psychologist living in Los Angeles. He's only in his early thirties, but as the book opens, he's "retired," having worked himself into a frenzy and then chucked it all.

It's an ironic round-trip. He was able to become a man of leisure because his considerable efforts generated a sizable income, which he invested in California real estate in its boom years. This brought him a windfall that gave him the option to walk away from what started it all.

But he's now restless with his jogging, hot tubs, and cultivating the ultimate tan. He succumbs to the urging of a detective with the Los Angeles Police Department to become involved in a difficult case, one where a brutal double murder was witnessed by a traumatized seven-year-old girl.

Alex's girlfriend doesn't like what's happening to him as he gets deeply into the case. She sees a disturbing pattern: "Now you're like a—a man possessed . . . I talk and your mind is somewhere else . . . you're going back to the bad old days."

Alex admits to himself: "There was something to that. The last few mornings have found me waking up early with a taut sense of urgency in my gut, the old obsessive drive to take care of business. Funny thing was, I didn't want to let go of it."

Burning Out

Make no mistake about it, burnout is a loss, a big one. It's a loss of caring, resulting from a lot of little losses that have gone ignored. These add up, and gradually one becomes ineffective, often without recognizing it. A burned-out person has to be told by others that something's missing, or be asked, "Is something wrong?"

Alex's drastic exit from his vocational calling was evidence that he wasn't able to maintain a sense of balance. I think he's going to be just fine, but for now, with the development of the story, we're prone to worry that he hasn't learned from his mistake, and his losses are going to mount.

Hanging in There

Clearly, the answer to the question should be "sometimes/ seldom." Amending our actions when we encounter little losses gives us the balance that at this point Alex lacks. It's what allows us to hang in there with a sense of purpose rather than throw out the baby with the bathwater.

Learning and growing require elasticity, a continuous cycle of moving forward and then falling back. An either-or attitude of full speed forward, all work or all play, is asking for trouble. In its permanence, the ocean offers just the right analogy as we watch it onshore: approach, thrust, rest, recede.

TAKE ACTION

1. Regroup. Let in a little light and air. You'll discover ways you've been missing the point.
2. Avoid either-or options. These are extreme and further underscore a lack of balance. All work makes Jack a dull boy, but so does all play. Selective retreat, not all-out escape, offers the best opportunity for renewed insights for your life's tasks.

64

POISED IN DEFEAT

Q: Are you a bad loser?

A: Usually/Often _____
Sometimes/Seldom _____

Yesterday I had lunch with a remarkable executive. At age forty-two, he's a contender for the chief executive position of one of the nation's most-respected large corporations.

I call him a contender because the current CEO has told him point-blank that's what he is. But he's not. He knows it, I know it, the CEO knows it, and the real contender probably knows it as well.

For some years he's wanted the job badly, but he now realizes he won't get it. Why? Because his style doesn't fit his corporation's culture. He came into this company as an outsider at the age of thirty-five to run a small, struggling division. He took the job at a lower salary than he was offered elsewhere because he admired this company and thought he could do something distinctive with this fledgling business.

He has. He's increased sales over tenfold and profits fifteenfold. His results are extraordinary—so superior to those of his peers running the company's other divisions that any CEO, for fear of embarrassing himself, would have to consider him a contender for the top spot in the hierarchy.

Outstanding results are not new to this man. I got acquainted with him ten years ago when he signed up for one of my strengths-development workshops, which I described earlier in Chapter 14. At age thirty-two he was already executive vice president of a company that, although much smaller than the corporation he works for today, was the largest in its business niche.

Green Ears

Many executives in corporate life like to delude themselves by thinking they're entrepreneurs. However, let them find themselves on the street as a result of some management purge or cost-reduction cutback, and you'll see them thrown into a panic. Ask the outplacement consultants how many of these people could make it without "mother company," and they'll tell you: almost none.

My idea of an entrepreneur is someone who sells his house, moves into a mobile home, and uses the proceeds from the sale of his house to buy or lease a small factory to make what he wants to sell to the world. How many executives do you know who are prepared to take that kind of risk?

Entrepreneurs are also a little weird. They act funny. They're mold-breakers, mavericks of the first order. They don't follow rules well, have peculiar ideas, and ask embarrassing questions, such as "Why can't we do that?" My friend, speaking of himself in his company, says, "I'm the guy with green ears!"

Now Biding His Time

You guessed it, this man is one of the rare breed who's able to succeed in an establishment, pinstripe company, but who at heart is an entrepreneur. He wears sports coats to work in his midtown Manhattan office, while his peers wouldn't be caught dead in other than three-piece suits. He's noisy, they're sophisticated. He's dying for recognition, they snicker while wishing they could accomplish what he does.

He's sanguine about all this now. He's lost the race and knows that the answer to the question should be "sometimes/seldom." He also knows, therefore, that the other guy is better for this company.

My friend has helped its stock soar, though, and in a couple of years will walk away with several million dollars from exercised stock options. He won't have to move into a mobile home when he starts *his* business.

TAKE ACTION

1. When you lose, don't rant and rave.
2. Bide your time. A bigger game is still ahead.

65

THE SECRET OF MARIO'S TENACITY

Q: **When adversity strikes, do you believe that things will eventually go your way?**

A: Usually/Often _____
Sometimes/Seldom _____

COOPER ROLLOW, VETERAN *Chicago Tribune* sportswriter, was conducting a postmortem of the 71st Indianapolis 500, one of the world's largest, most spectacular sporting events, won by Al Unser, Sr.

This was the race Mario Andretti was supposed to win. The savvy driver had the right car, and all signs pointed to his being untouchable. Wrote Rollow:

> Andretti, who had led for 170 laps and seemed ready to rid him-self of his 20-year-old Indy jinx in a new Lola Chevrolet he had labeled perfect, suddenly slowed after the 177th lap. Gone, once again, were Andretti's hopes of winning his first Indy 500 since 1969.

A small fuel-metering part did him in. Andretti reacted to his defeat this way:

> I always have a cautious optimism. I've lost a lot of races I was leading. But I've never gone that far into a race and broken down like that. Usually after 450 miles they don't break down. This was really weird.

Despite disappointment for himself and his crew, he neverthe-less continued:

> I don't want to talk about any jinxes. All your talk about jinxes you can keep to yourself. We had a great month, and nobody got hurt. And next year, hopefully, if I come back I'll press on to win it again. One of these days it's got to go my way.

Hope

Whether Mario Andretti ever wins another Indy 500, he's shown himself in these few words to be a champion. He realizes that he is not in total control of his destiny, but he demonstrates mastery of the elements of his life that are in his hands.

By saying "hopefully, if I come back . . ." he indicates that further competition is not a sure thing. There is, mainly, the matter of raising the sizable financing for entering the race. The new car and its developmental costs. The grueling hours of training. The multiple crew. All this for a driver thought in some circles to be plagued with bad luck. It won't be easy.

Whatever self-doubts he had as a competitor have likely faded by now, and his statement "I'll press on to win it again" says where his heart is. This alone tells us that his spirit will prevail in the end.

Hope is made of desire plus expectation. To have hope is to stalk something, believing its possibility. Can there be any question that, if left to his own devices, Andretti will be aiming for next year's pole position?

Going My Way

The real secret to Andretti's tenacity is his outright rejection of fate being his permanent enemy. None of us with any smarts ignores the element of chance in our lives. Undeniably, there are events and convergences that can work against us.

But reacting well to those losses by learning from them is what eventually forces things to go our way. Andretti's comments reflect extraordinary poise and depth. Though he may never again win at Indianapolis, it's clear that he's set up to be a winner at whatever he decides to do with the rest of his life. His "time" is coming.

As I'm sure you've guessed by now, the answer to the question should be "usually/often."

TAKE ACTION

1. Acknowledge your annoyance with having to accept tenacity as a requirement for consistent success. After

all, it's far preferable to think there's an angle ... some
guideline ... a technique you can call on.

2. Then strap yourself back into harness when facing some
    disagreeable prospect, accepting the fact that often the
    only margin of victory is no more than just your being
    determined to wear the bastards down.

Note: Shortly before this book went to press, the 72nd Indianapolis 500 was run.
Mario, his son Michael, his nephew John all competed in the race. None of them
won. "We're all young yet," said the 47-year-old Mario.

66

LAUGHING AT OURSELVES

Q: **Do you laugh when the joke's on you?**

A: Usually/Often _____
Sometimes/Seldom _____

I USE "the joke's on you" here as a figure of speech. It refers to those times when for some reason or because of some event, you've looked foolish. None of us are exempt from these occasions, so handling them with poise is of paramount importance for minimizing the damage. The answer to the question, therefore, should be "usually/often."

Denying Our Humanity

Many executives regularly put barriers between themselves and their associates by being unwilling to laugh at themselves. These barriers result from the executive saying by his humorless reaction that he doesn't make mistakes. Oh, he may claim that of course he makes mistakes, but when it comes to specific circumstances, such admission is seldom forthcoming.

To deny making mistakes is to deny our humanity, a denial that cannot be interpreted as anything but absurd and grandiose. And it reaps the opposite of its intended effects—namely, a hope by (and in some cases, a helping hand from) onlookers to see us cut down to size.

To laugh at ourselves is to laugh *with* others and benefit from camaraderie and fellowship. Not to do so is to be laughed *at* behind our backs and experience separation. Our subordinates, in particular, need to see such vulnerability from us. Just like us, if not more so, they worry over their performance. They *know* they screw up. It helps them to see that their boss does too, and that when he does, he can handle it with a laugh.

Better Late Than Never

Even better than laughing when the joke's on you is pointing out errors and foibles of yours that have escaped the attention of others. And a final saving grace—an action that can convert damage to your advantage—is laughing at yourself today, even though you couldn't yesterday.

I have a client and friend, president of a food company with $4 billion in annual sales, who is good at blending all three of these behaviors. He is particularly disarming in admitting errors and shortcomings others haven't noticed, and is usually quick to join in the laughter when it's at his expense. Nonetheless, there have been occasions when I've been in his presence and seen that others thought he was joining in such laughter, but I know him well enough to realize that he was not. His grin took on a crookedness that told me he was hurting.

Game as he was, and as much as I admired him for it, he made it clear that no matter how much we ought to, we're simply not always *able* to laugh at ourselves, not authentically anyway. What I admire even more in my friend is his showing me that given a little time, he can replace those hollow laughs with genuine mirth. His people love him for this.

TAKE ACTION

1. Think of three events in the past year when your performance drew laughter from your associates and that laughter raised your hackles.
2. Your indignation fooled nobody. Don't be overt about it, but find a way to let the people involved know that those were times you took yourself too seriously. In so doing, and by guarding against repeating such pretentions from now on, you'll reduce needless barriers between you and them.

67

APPLYING
THE NEEDLE

Q: **Do you needle your associates
with critical hints rather than
stating criticism directly?**

A: Usually/Often _____
Sometimes/Seldom _____

It wasn't an important meeting by any means. Routine, actually. And Karen wasn't expected to make a report or do anything special. This was just the weekly meeting of the tax department at her accounting firm, where all the managers talked informally about the progress of their client assignments and tried to help one another out with any problems.

The camaraderie was always good. Karen felt especially welcome at these sessions and was proud of that, because as the only female manager in the group, she had earned her way into this male club with her performance.

Karen had been an average student in college, but had passed the CPA exam the first time she tried. Some of her fellow students who had done better than she in the classroom weren't as able, and had to repeat the exam once or twice. Karen had taken naturally to taxes, and the word bandied about the office on her was "creative." In tax work, that's a precious possession.

So she was stunned at what happened in the meeting. At one point when everyone was laughingly commiserating with George, who was lamenting his trials with a prima donna client, Ken turned to Karen and said, "Let's ask our Egyptian princess about that. By the way, Karen, with all those bracelets you wear, how do you lift your arms?"

Gales of laughter. Karen faked a laugh too, blushed uncontrollably, and babbled a response. But she was cut to the quick and could have crawled into a hole.

Hints Don't Work

Ken is the culprit here. But let me not be overly judgmental in my finger pointing. We all engage in such needling. "What's more," We might say, "it worked. Message sent. Message received." The next day Karen came into the office with her arms free of all the clanking baggage. She was good-natured about it, too. When she ran into a bunch of the guys, she raised her arms and exclaimed, "See, guys, all clean!"

But what I see is that Karen is terrific at absorbing a hostile barb. One overnight to lick her wounds was all she needed before coming back to mix it up with her peers.

Moreover, the larger message that ought to have been sent, wasn't. So there's no way it could have been received. *You know*: There's also this wild way Karen wears her hair. Then there are her loud clothes. And those sandals—my god, where does she find those goofy shoes? Our clients have to be wondering.

Perhaps the point I want to make with you is obscured by my choosing Karen, who is exemplary in her good-natured response. Many people would not only fail to receive the larger message, but resent the needling and perhaps rebel against it. Others might simply think, "Why should I change my wardrobe because of a rude joker like Ken?"

Caring About Karen

This chapter isn't about the morality of dress codes. They exist and always have. The Comanche tribe had one. Hippies had one. J. Walter Thompson has one. Morgan Guaranty Bank has one, and so does Karen's accounting firm.

Karen is, as I've said, a gem. She's a technical whiz and has shown her emotional depth many times over. She has a great sense of humor (unlike Ken) and knows how to work well with people.

Karen doesn't need the needle. She'll respond perfectly to someone who cares enough to overcome the embarrassment of being direct about the entire way she presents herself physically. She's proof that the answer to the question should be "sometimes/seldom."

TAKE ACTION

1. Recall the last time you were needled. Wasn't there a better way?
2. Next time you're about to stick in it, stop. There *is* a better way.

68

CATCHING YOUR BALANCE

Q: Do you accept the comical in yourself without hurting your own feelings?

A: Usually/Often _____
Sometimes/Seldom _____

"YOU POOR FOLKS . You're stuck with a CEO—yours truly—who thought building that $15 million plant three years ago was the greatest idea since the wheel. Now we've got to shut it down. Schools are lousy in that God-forsaken town, and no executive's family wants to live there. Our quality there stinks and we've had two product recalls. We've done nothing but lose our shirts while supposedly saving money. Watch me. Learn from me. Put what you see to work and someday you can be a smart CEO just like me.

"George," the CEO deadpans, pointing to his vice president of operations, one of his seven top executives sitting around the oval conference table at the Monday morning staff meeting, "where were you when I really needed you? All you said when I kept insisting that we build this damn thing was that it was the dumbest idea you ever heard. Ya gotta speak plainer, man, so I know what you mean."

By now, of course, everyone around the table is smiling and chuckling. But not guffawing, mind you, because one sizable chunk of money has gone down the tube, and that wreaks havoc with the balance sheet of this midsize company. Not only that, although feelings ran high in the disputes over this project gone wrong, the respect these people have for one another is such that they refuse to split themselves into winners laughing at losers.

A Bad Call

In one way, to be sure, they all were losers. But in another, they all came out winners too. It's clear from the spirit of the meeting, in which the CEO pokes fun at himself, that this management team is marked by a residue of goodwill.

The fact is, the CEO had been absurd in his unrelenting pursuit of building this plant. While numerous red flags were thrown up by research data and opinions of several of his staff—most forcefully by his vice president of operations—he lost all objectivity in this case and rammed his decision through.

Yet because he is the kind of person he is and has been, he

lost little in the eyes of his people. To them, he only proved he was human. Although his record of growth is outstanding, this time around he made a bad call.

Delayed Reaction

The first year of the plant's operation, there were the usual start-up problems. The second year things got even worse. The CEO got a little touchy now and then, but basically put a good face on things. The third year he realized he'd blown it.

Very few of us can laugh off our big mistakes when they're fresh, and the CEO was no exception. But some people can *never* laugh them off and that's deadly. Where the CEO caught his balance was recognizing his comical behavior, acknowledging it among some of those who were hurt by it, but not letting it get them or him down.

The answer to the question should be "usually/often"—even if it takes a while.

TAKE ACTION

1. So...what you did was absurd. You made a fool of yourself. It stings, but live with it; give it a breather.
2. Later, let yourself know you were buying time. Then laugh with those among whom you blundered. It will make you stronger and increase your self-esteem.

69

GREEKS
BEARING GIFTS

Q: Is your laughter nervous laughter?

A: Usually/Often _____
Sometimes/Seldom _____

A PRIEST WITH a twinkle in his eye once told me that he wished he could preach a Mother's Day homily to women magically transformed into the frame of mind of a few hours earlier, on Saturday night. "Better yet," he said, "would be if we could somehow recapture the setting, see most of them having a good time, living it up, instead of the faces of decorum that I address."

Last Monday, I flew back fairly late from a business trip. By the time I got home and showered, it was later still, but my wife and I went out for a yet later supper at our favorite Greek restaurant.

When we arrived, most diners were finishing up. Near the end of our meal, the place empty except for us, in walked a large, noisy group of eight or ten people all speaking Greek. They knew the owner, were seated quickly, and ordered a few bottles of wine.

It soon was clear that their "noise" was mirth. They were having a good time. This was some kind of celebration. One of the men strode over to the grand piano and began to play a beautiful Greek melody. Shortly he was joined by a woman who sang three or four lusty songs. Though we couldn't understand their words, we enjoyed them and her fully. Someone in the group noticed our pleasure and sent the waiter over to get our drink order.

"Ouzo," we said, and from several tables across the room we joined in the party by lifting our glasses.

Belly Laughs

The next morning in the office my thoughts turned to the kinds of laughter we often hear in the corridors and boardrooms of business. Then I remembered the priest. Wouldn't it be nice if in our work we could laugh the way we laughed with the Greeks?

A real laugh comes from down below. It has depth. Athletes, actors, quality vocalists, meditators of all stripes, and voice therapists hammer away at the necessity of breathing from the diaphragm for full functioning. "Belly breathing" they call it. A real laugh is a belly laugh. That doesn't mean it has to be loud. It's not obnoxious either. Rather, it's contagious.

Throat Laughs

Most of us laugh from the throat. Infants and young children laugh from the belly. And they don't laugh unless something is funny. We laugh a lot when things aren't funny, and when we do, we laugh from our throats. Most comedians aren't funny, and they laugh from their throats. And when we laugh at their jokes, we laugh from our throats. Constricted, whiny, hollow, nervous.

When we're scared, our breath is short. When we laugh scared, it's obvious to anyone with a measure of insight. The correct answer to the question, therefore, should be "sometimes/seldom."

TAKE ACTION

1. Buy and read *Mentally Tough* by Dr. James E. Loehr and Peter J. McLaughlin (New York: Evans, 1986, $8.95). It will help you gain control of your life and develop your poise. Pay particular attention to its chapter on breathing.
2. Buy and read *Change Your Voice, Change Your Life* by Dr. Morton Cooper (New York: Perennial, 1984, $6.95). This book will help you get control of your voice, an ability that most people lack. It also offers tips on correct breathing.

Both books are outstanding, short, and easy to read.

70

PANDERING FOR LAUGHS

Q: **Do you joke with people to maintain your distance from them?**

A: Usually/Often _____
    Sometimes/Seldom _____

EACH MORNING WHEN at home, I wake up to a program on a pop music station. The station plays rock classics throughout its round-the-clock schedule. I like the music. My automatic alarm and radio dial stay tuned to this station so that I can enjoy it whenever attending to my preparatory chores at both the beginning and the end of the day.

What I don't enjoy is the format of the morning show. It is centered around comedy and designed to compete with a growing number of rock stations where antics and zaniness are put on the air in a misguided attempt to entertain.

One of the co-hosts of the show is a comedian who appears regularly in a local comedy club. Have you seen these clubs popping up in our major cities? They exist to provide budding comics with audiences before whom they can perfect their acts. I wouldn't go near them. They must be dreadful places.

What's less funny than a typical stand-up comedian's string of gags? Not much. Such comedians' pandering for laughs is, instead, embarrassing, and their performances inspire more sadness than happiness in many of us. I become more aware of this as I listen to this co-host in the mornings.

Joking Isn't Humor

The reason Bill Cosby and Garrison Keillor (and others like them) are funny in their stand-up routines is that they don't tell *jokes*. They tell *stories*—stories we laugh at genuinely because we're laughing at ourselves. We can see our foibles in these stories. Sooner or later we're part of the action. We're included because we always can identify with one of Cosby's or Keillor's characters.

Candid Camera made us laugh uproariously not with desperate jokes at somebody's expense, but because as we watched others "caught in the act of being themselves," we knew that "they" were "we." We were there, or could have been. We were included. *We were able to see the comical in ourselves without hurting our own feelings*. That's humor.

Joking Creates Distance

The executive suite needs humor but most often gets joking. We need more of the attitude that we're all in this life together, but what we have instead is finger pointing—with a snicker or guffaw attached, of course. Phony smiles and fake laughs (heh-heh-heh, hawr-hawr-hawr) abound.

There's a more subtle form of joking, too, that creates distance between people and hinders their communication with one another. We see it most in that executive who never gets serious. This is the one who claims he's lightening up the situation when things are getting too tense. Usually, this means things are getting too tense for *him*.

Actually, there's a little bit of this guy in all of us. When our actions are called into question by someone, we're inclined to put distance between us and that person by making light of him or the subject somehow. In the process we fail to learn from the situation by facing it squarely. We also fail to foster a relationship.

For all these reasons, the answer to the question should be "sometimes/seldom."

TAKE ACTION

1. Monitor your laughs for a week. Note whether they're an expression of mirth or anxiety.
2. If you're the habitual meeting "lightener-upper," consider changing your role.

71

LEARNING FROM FAILURE

Q: **Do you blame circumstances for your failures?**

A: Usually/Often _____
Sometimes/Seldom _____

"**F**AILURE" IS A word that jars us. The mere sound has an impact on our bodies. Whenever we're engaged in any activity we deem important, and the judgment of failure is applied against it from some quarter we also deem important, we recoil and try to dissociate ourselves from the failure as quickly as possible.

The Blaming Disposition

Because being identified with failure is so offensive to most of us, we're often tempted to blame circumstances rather than our performance for its existence. While it's human enough, and therefore forgivable to do so, this bit of self-deception keeps us from learning from our mistakes. This means that the answer to the question should be "sometimes/seldom."

Of course, there are times when circumstances can erupt in detrimental and unforeseen ways that prevent us from accomplishing what we set out to do. But it is at least equally true that events called "unforeseen" could have been seen if we'd taken off our blinders, and those that "erupt" might well have been managed if we had prepared better.

The trap to avoid is accommodating the blaming disposition in ourselves or making this evasion of personal responsibility *habitual*. Whenever we let ourselves off the hook this way, it is just that much easier to make the same errors the next time. Who can deny how effortlessly we can adopt the complainer's role? And as we do, we invite the failure we attempt to avoid.

Reinterpreting Failure

Part of our difficulty with failure is refusing to see its positive aspects. In our inclination to put as much distance between us and it as fast as we can, we obliterate any opportunity to have it contribute to our emotional development and job competence.

This was brought home to me last week when I met for two

days with the top management of the international group of one of our major drug companies.

At one point we were discussing how tenacity is critical to any executive's sustained success. One of the executives present, noting his own part in recommending a $10 million investment that became a mistake, said, "You have to wrestle failure all the way down to the ground. You mustn't run from it, but stay with it. Eventually, you'll be able to reinterpret it."

What great wisdom! This executive was telling us what he learned by his willingness to remain associated with a colossal failure. He insisted on an "autopsy" on how he and his associates came to make such a bad decision. He said he believes this taught him how to make more high-stakes good ones in the future.

I agree. I'm sure it did.

TAKE ACTION

1. Think of a mistake you made recently that you have avoided acknowledging. Emphatically say to yourself twenty times, "I failed." Own your mistake. Then notice how the world doesn't come to an end!

2. Wrestle that failure to the ground. Dissect it. Let yourself know what you learned from it. Celebrate your increased wisdom. Encourage your associates to engage in this two-step process. Moreover, keep this exercise in waiting, ready for those inevitable failures that lie ahead.

72

A BLOWHARD EXERCISE

Q: **Are you a practitioner of the philosophy, "If it ain't broke, don't fix it?"**

A: Usually/Often _____
Sometimes/Seldom _____

PEOPLE KEEP GIVING me books written by Masaaki Imai, the Japanese management consultant. My first benefactor some years ago was Dave Buyher. Buyher is CEO of the North American high-tech medical products businesses for Smiths Industries, a London-based company.

Buyher, a friend, client, and first-rate profit-center executive, had spent a lot of time in Japan and wanted me to be aware of Japanese business philosophies. To coach me, he gave me a copy of Imai's tight little book, *Never Take Yes for an Answer*. I enjoyed it thoroughly.

My second benefactor was Tom Horton, CEO of the American Management Association. When I was visiting with him in his office recently, he tapped a book with his right forefinger and told me it was one of the best books he'd ever read on management. Then he gave it to me. That book was Imai's *Kaizen*.

"Kaizen" is a Japanese word that means gradual, unending improvement, doing little things better, setting and achieving ever-higher standards. Tom Horton is right on the mark. *Kaizen* is an outstanding book, and I underscore his opinion. Although many American executives are tired of reading about Japan, they can benefit from reading *Kaizen* and applying its message.

Polluted Message

That message gets polluted somewhat, however, by book-jacket copy, which states that *Kaizen*'s main thrust is to fix something "even if it ain't broke." This is a misinterpretation of what the book is really about.

Tom Peters offers the same view these days. In his book *Thriving on Chaos*, he too says we should "fix it even if it ain't broke." Moreover, just a few years ago, the General Electric Company was touting its manufacturing services business with expensive full-page ads in *The Wall Street Journal*, *The New York Times*, and other well-known publications that admonished, "If it ain't broke, fix it."

Now, certainly I get the point of this overstatement, and so do you. Further, we both agree, I'm sure, with its intent: "Let's be certain that what we make or do, not only works but works well." In a word, let's generate *quality*. Our well-ensconced thoughts on preventive maintenance enter the picture as well, along with such wise old admonitions as "A stitch in time saves nine." After all this, however, the statement itself still ends up being a blowhard exercise.

Vigilance Where Needed

Consider this parable: Three days in a row, an employee left a foundry with a wheelbarrow full of straw. Each day the security guard stopped him at the door, rummaged through the straw, and finding nothing, sent him on his way. The fourth day, the guard stopped him and exclaimed, "Look, you're driving me crazy. I promise I won't report you, but please just tell me what you're stealing." The worker replied, "Wheelbarrows."

Fixing what ain't broke is vigilance where it ain't needed. It's concentrating on the straw instead of what's missing from the toolshed. It's the sideshow rather than the main event. It's the distraction rather than the centerpiece. It's the child in school who's always getting organized to study, but never getting around to studying. It's an invitation to meddle. It's razzle-dazzle gridiron maneuvers without basic blocking and tackling.

Several chapters in this book allude to the fact that most of us have more to do than sufficient time to do it. Priority setting says the answer to the question should be "usually/often."

TAKE ACTION

1. Do first things first, second things hardly ever.
2. When you do something, do it right the first time. Then it won't break.

73

BEATING BAD BREAKS

Q: **Are you a "hard luck" executive?**

A: Usually/Often _____
Sometimes/Seldom _____

JOE BTFSPLK WAS that unforgettable character in the late Al Capp's comic strip—*Li'l Abner*—who walked around with a black cloud over his head. You might say he had an attitude problem. Wherever he went, he made sure that life rained on the parade.

We've all run into executives just like Joe during the course of our careers, but by virtue of being an executive recruiter, it's likely that I've seen more than my share. One telltale sign of such people is their possession of a résumé that shows a string of jobs—all lasting three years or less—with different companies. Such executives aren't tolerated for long.

Many of them get to be labeled hard-luck cases, but don't believe this explanation for failure for one second. Their problem isn't luck at all, but—as I've hinted—attitude.

New proof for this old truism can be drawn from figures in my recent book *Inside Corporate America*. In this book made up of almost 400 questions put to over a thousand executives in thirteen identified corporations, it's clear that the most successful ones do not consider luck to have had a significant impact on their job success.

Good Luck

Only 8 percent of the 515 top executives in this study say that good luck has had a "very positive" impact on their careers. On the other hand, the credit given to maintaining various attitudes for job success offers a marked contrast.

Among these same top executives, 49 percent say positive attitude itself has had a "very positive" impact on their careers. That number for rebounding from adversity is 34 percent. For high expectations for your own achievements it's 42 percent. For persuasiveness it's 48 percent. For drive it's 61 percent. For perceptiveness about people it's also 48 percent.

Management styles based on attitude produced these numbers for very positive impact on top executives' careers: loyalty 49 percent; knowing how to set priorities and stick with them 58 percent; honesty 75 percent; adhering to deadlines 39 percent; and encouraging your subordinates 44 percent.

I could cite more categories, but these should suffice to make the point. Moreover, I have great confidence in these numbers because the 1,086 executives who returned this confidential questionnaire constituted 93 percent of those invited to do so.

Bad Luck

As mentioned in Chapter 65, no one with a jot of intelligence denies the element of chance that exists in life. But the more critical issues are, first, how we can pattern our lives to create the likelihood of good breaks, and second, how we can spot those growth-blocking attitudes we nurture that are likely to lead to bad breaks.

If we will be vigilant with these critical tasks, we won't be known as hard-luck executives, and we'll be able to answer the question resolutely "sometimes/seldom."

TAKE ACTION

1. Benjamin Disraeli said, "The secret of success in life is for a man to be ready for his opportunity when it comes." Get yourself ready.
2. Write down one attitude you nurse that's an excuse, rather than an explanation, for some recent failure. Reach for a bright red felt-tip pen and draw a line through what you've written.

74

FLEEING FORWARD

Q: **Are you hesitant to act on your private judgments?**

A: Usually/Often _____
Sometimes/Seldom _____

THE SUMMER OF 1955, an interlude before I entered college, was a rich one. I had a terrific girlfriend and a job. The former was more important, of course, but I also needed the money for school.

My job was working the front desk, from three to eleven, of a brand-new YMCA that had opened in our community. I greeted visitors and inquirers, and I directed people to the membership office, cafeteria, gym, pool, and various self-improvement classes. I registered guests, collected rents from regular tenants, and even learned to operate the switchboard.

I enjoyed my job, but the Y was a bustling place in those days, and I always was happy to see Bud, the night man and my relief, walk through the door each night at 10:45.

Bud was a puzzle to me. He wasn't handsome, but good-looking enough, good-natured, slim, dark-haired, a plain but neat dresser, single, and about age thirty-five. He held a master's degree in history and seemed (to this eighteen-year-old, at least) to be unusually well read and articulate.

Contrary to my suspicions, Bud had never been a teacher, nor had he gone on to school beyond his master's. Nor did he have career plans from here on. He was just the night man, that's all, a job he'd had for eight years, and he felt no need to make changes. Not a drifter, obviously enough, but certainly an idler.

Marginal Types

Since that summer, I've encountered several Buds. I imagine you have too. They're not to be ignored, because they're charming, articulate, and usually well educated and abreast of things. It's only later, after you learn more about them, that you find out that they're not fully using their gifts.

The social veneer that allows them to perform well initially in a person-to-person encounter wears through quickly to reveal a life that is somehow lived in the shadows. They are marginal types who would be well placed in a Joyce Carol Oates novel.

One wonders how many are middle children, squeezed out by the pace setters before them and the overcomers behind them.

One Step Beyond

The Buds are an extreme picture, and although they arouse our curiosity, understanding how they got to be that way is beyond our competence and purposes here. Yet it is instructive to acknowledge that there's a shade of their behavior in ours every time we reach a judgment and fail to act on it. Whatever prompted Bud's low expectations also feeds ours. His lack of volition may blanket his whole life, while ours is fragmentary, but I'm convinced that they're part of the same continuum on which we misuse our gifts.

Jacques Maritain, French philosopher and theologian, declared, "The man of courage flees forward." His observation underscores that the answer to the question should be "sometimes/seldom." The Buds of this world are thought of as victims. But those who flee forward, we know from experience, are the ones who make their breaks.

TAKE ACTION

1. Don't idle. Make yourself fully aware of what you believe on some issue you face. "This is what I think!" Then move.
2. Sit tight, however, if inaction is the indicated action. A clear head while all others are spinning wheels is, to be sure, fleeing forward.

75

THE PRICE
OF BECOMING
ENVIABLE

Q: **Do you enviously watch
others do what you could do?**

A: Usually/Often _____
Sometimes/Seldom _____

Y ESTERDAY I ARRIVED home from out of town in the early afternoon. I got into my workout clothes (which means I stripped down to my underwear) and went to our home gym (which means spare bedroom with stationary bike and TV).

There I usually do my rudimentary calisthenics and huff and puff away on the Schwinn Air-Dyne while watching *The MacNeil/Lehrer NewsHour*. But yesterday, because of the early time, I caught *The Phil Donahue Show*, and what a treat it was.

Donahue's guests were four black giants. Singers. Greats. Joe Williams, Carmen McRae, Billy Eckstine, and Nancy Wilson. Of course, Donahue did his thing, which he does so well, and the studio audience and viewers got a piece of these folks. But he also had the good sense to have them sing. Each one performed and, my oh my, how they put across a song.

Like most adults, I've seen and enjoyed all four of these entertainers over the years, but permit me one memory. Seeing Joe Williams took me back to 1957, when I was a college sophomore. Williams was singing with The Count Basie Band, and a friend and I went to one of their appearances at Riverside-Brookfield High School in suburban Chicago.

One of their songs that night—"Old Man River"—has stood out in my mind ever since. One reason was Joe Williams's upbeat tempo of this classic in his rich, powerful baritone. Another was a long solo between Williams's vocals by Basie's drummer. I couldn't believe it, nor would you. Have you ever heard "Old Man River" played on the *drums*? I have.

Envied Artists

Entertainers of this quality are the envy of us all. And there's a lesson in that. But the lesson isn't that we covet their specific gifts. For example, I don't want to sing like Mel Torme or dance like Gene Kelly. Oh, it would be nice to play trumpet like Wynton Marsalis, or flute like Herbie Mann, or piano like Dave Brubeck, but that's not where my heart is.

The lesson in our envy of mold-breaking entertainers is that they are *captivating*. They are taken seriously. They win over attention. They make us feel what they feel. We stop what we're doing and thinking and get into their agenda, their program. They have the "information," and persuade us with it. They are consummate communicators. The message sent is the message received.

Risk and Pain

Well, what executive honest with himself wouldn't want to be so captivating on the job? Yet wishing won't make it so. Donahue's guests know that. What risks they've taken on stage before large audiences and flopped! How low they must have felt now and then throughout their distinguished careers. Then how bland the audience response was on those occasions when they played it safe or couldn't give of themselves.

What about the odds and bad breaks they overcame, and the hurts they absorbed, particularly because they're black? Billy Eckstine said it made him mad when he was called "The Sepia Sinatra."

What I think he meant was that it hurt.

But the point is that he and Donahue's other three guests kept working anyway to realize their dreams, instead of giving up and envying others whose roads seemed smoother. These singers know that the answer to the question should be "sometimes/seldom."

TAKE ACTION

1. Be like Donahue's guests. Don't envy. Be *envied*.
2. To be envied, work like hell, risk your psyche, endure the flops, and put the bad luck behind you. In short, pay the price. There's no other way.

76

WORK OF ART, ART OF WORK

Q: **Do you draw praise from your peers and higher-level managers for your work?**

A: Usually/Often _____
Sometimes/Seldom _____

LAST WEEK I saw a master at work. The master is Robert Shaw, famed founder and conductor of The Robert Shaw Chorale and music director of The Atlanta Symphony Orchestra—a post he's held for 20 years.

I grew up on Robert Shaw, or at least learned about him in my early teens. My father hailed from Alabama—though he lived all his adult life in the North—and I made a hero of myself one year by buying him the Robert Shaw Chorale album *Songs of the South*. How he loved it, and so did I, as he listened to it again and again over the years.

Shaw's honors include seven Grammys; three ASCAP awards for service to contemporary music; honorary degrees and awards from over thirty U.S. colleges, universities, and foundations; and the first Guggenheim Fellowship ever awarded to a conductor. Later in 1988, shortly before his announced retirement, he'll receive the Gold Baton award—the nation's highest honor for distinguished service to music and the arts.

Shaw's performance last week was two-part. He conducted a choir in Schubert's *Mass in G*, but before that he delivered a lecture entitled "Worship and the Arts."

In describing art, he said it is marked by four qualities: (1) purity of purpose, (2) historical perspective, (3) craftsmanship, and (4) revelation. May he forgive me, but as he spoke, my thoughts turned to what we in business sometimes call the art of management.

A Lofty Message

Actually, I don't think Shaw would be upset with me at all, because he clearly views the world as an evolutionary unfolding of man's expression of his gifts through his art. And it seems obvious that there is an evolutionary unfolding in the world of work—from CEO to the last person on the third shift to leave the plant—whereby there is a passion to bring what is uniquely one's own gifts to the job.

This notion may rightly be called lofty, but it is undeniably in process and inexorable. We're less apologetic and embarrassed these days to voice our concerns about *purity of purpose*. Ethics is as hot a topic as any in business. "Management by values" is a watchword in many companies.

Historical perspective has come to the fore with our absorption with corporate culture. It's not enough to blithely talk about and wish for what we and our corporations might be. We must give long, hard thought to where we have been and what we're becoming. Shaw dealt with *revelation* by defining art as "the flesh made word." Now that's a really nifty little twist! The more we experience our work as a calling, as performance for its own sake and as a quality offering for those on its receiving end, the more it says and the more power it has.

Craftsmanship

Shaw's third quality of art, *craftsmanship*, I've left until last. If craftsmanship is the vehicle for expressing one's unique gifts, then the desire for that expression is its fuel. Craftsmanship is the refinement of one's gifts, and that lifelong undertaking cannot be sustained unless one gives a name to and dedicates himself to his heart's desire.

Genuine praise for our work is generated among our associates only when we see that work as a "festival of art." Sounds wacky, eh? Try it. You'll like it. The answer to the question should be "usually/often."

TAKE ACTION

1. With all the scratching, climbing, straining, and envying, an executive often loses touch with his heart's desire. Call time-out.
2. Your work demands your heart's desire if you are to excel over the long haul. Give a name to it. Then give yourself to what you name.

77

WATCHING YOUR COMPANY'S FEET

Q: Do you ponder the unarticulated goals of your corporation?

A: Usually/Often _____
Sometimes/Seldom _____

While having lunch with a banker friend recently, a man responsible for the human resources function at his bank, I asked him what he thought of the corporate culture phenomenon. He thought a moment and said it was a "wave that had washed up on the shore and was now on its way back to sea."

Unarticulated Goals

I understand exactly what my friend means. The notion of corporate culture erupted as a fad with the publication in 1982 of the book entitled, predictably enough, *Corporate Cultures*. But let me say quickly that the authors themselves (Allan Kennedy and Terry Deal), are embarrassed at some of the silliness that came from their work. They tell the story of the CEO of a company who heard a presentation by them and then turned to his president and said, "This corporate culture thing is great. I want one by Monday morning."

While I agree with this perceptive banker that the faddish elements of the movement have about run their course, the idea behind it has shown itself to be remarkably persistent. For example, I have in my library at home a book written by Paul Meadows entitled *The Culture of Industrial Man*, published by The University of Nebraska Press in 1950.

I believe the reason for this persistence of the cultural approach, and our recurring fascination with it, is that we realize that rational management seldom gets the job done by itself. In addition, we need a perspective for understanding why things often don't go according to plan.

The value of the corporate culture movement is that it has taught us this: We don't know what makes our companies tick as much as we thought we did. And we're just beginning to sense that there are goals operating in our companies that we haven't been aware of fully.

Pondering Unarticulated Goals

I find it helpful to picture any corporation as two slightly over-lapping circles. One circle I label "rhetoric," the other "essence." Under the circle called rhetoric I write (1) intention, (2) apparent, and (3) mouth. Under the circle called essence, I write (1) goals, (2) hidden, and (3) feet.

The point of all this is fairly obvious: The circle called rhetoric represents that part of a corporation that spells out its avowed intentions. This includes its articulated goals and is apparent in such documents as the annual report, the long-range plan, advertising campaigns, and current slogans. This is the corporation's mouth.

The circle called essence represents that part of a corporation that although not fully understood, will not be denied, despite official rhetoric. It is the part that is made up of unarticulated (hidden) goals that translate to unshakable convictions. This is the corporation's feet. And where these feet walk is ultimately at least as important as where the mouth says they should be walking.

If we want to understand a corporation, we of course will listen to what issues from its mouth. But more importantly, we will study its feet. For that reason, the answer to the question should be "usually/often."

TAKE ACTION

1. Ask yourself: "Do I ever studiously wonder why things don't go according to plan?"
2. Pledge to watch your company's feet. Where they walk tells you what goals your company *really* is serving.

78

A REGIMEN FOR IDEAS

Q: Do you set your own performance goals without regard for your company's unarticulated goals?

A: Usually/Often _____
Sometimes/Seldom _____

Davidavid ogilvy is the Scotsman who, more than any other person, set the standards for taste and style in the field of advertising. He's founder of Ogilvy & Mather, the firm that currently ranks fourth in billings among all advertising agencies in the United States.

In 1963, Ogilvy published his classic *Confessions of an Advertising Man*. In it he writes: "I hear a great deal of music. I am on friendly terms with John Barleycorn. I take long hot baths. I garden. I go into retreat among the Amish. I watch birds. I go for long walks in the country. And I take frequent vacations, so that my brain can lie fallow—no golf, no cocktail parties, no tennis, no bridge, no concentration; only a bicycle."

He goes on to say that while he is thus employed doing nothing, ideas percolate that form the basis of his ads, then hastily notes that this mental meandering needs to be buttressed with "hard work, an open mind, and ungovernable curiosity."

In Chapter 77, I called attention to how the corporate culture movement has made it clear that we aren't fully aware of all the goals operating in our companies. Much earlier, in Chapter 42, I urged you to clarify for yourself what the big yes of your company is and get behind it.

Percolating Ideas

Ogilvy's unusual regimen for getting ideas to percolate in the service of selling products and services is illustrative of what must be done to be imaginative about our organizations and our place in them.

This is a foreign notion to most executives. The expression of an ungovernable curiosity, when present at all, is seldom a part of organizational thought. As reported in my recently published book *Inside Corporate America*, only a fourth of top executives see great benefit in being a "student of organizations."

There's no way to give words to the unarticulated goals of your corporation unless you're willing to accommodate the percolation of ideas. This leads to insights concerning what your corporation is about that has not been acknowledged by others.

Moreover, it provides the opportunity for you to set your own performance goals in harmony with that thrust—which, while not all that apparent, is nonetheless governing.

The requirement for you to apply your ungovernable curiosity to what truly governs means that the answer to the question should be "sometimes/seldom."

Hard Work

It's easy to rattle off goals. Words are cheap, and as the cliché says, the road to hell is paved with good intentions. What's hard, though, is to set a goal that may fly in the face of official rhetoric. Harder still is standing by it and making good on it when subject to cold stares or verbal abuse from associates or bosses.

I remember reading a piece in *Fortune* back in the early 1980s that described the corporate culture of the 3M Company. The writer pointed out that the worst that could be said about you if you worked there was that you killed an idea. He then went on to describe a technician who overcame working for a boss who, in this instance at least, risked being such a pariah.

This technician is an example of what I've been espousing. Fired for spending too much time to develop a product his boss thought was fruitless, he kept showing up, working without pay until he got it right.

He was reinstated, of course, and is today a hero. (The writer, as I recall, didn't say what happened to his boss.) By going against the grain, the technician got behind the big yes at 3M—innovation.

TAKE ACTION

1. You needn't copy Ogilvy, but build your own regimen for the percolation of ideas.
2. Steel yourself for the grief you'll face by occasionally going against the tide of official rhetoric.

79

BEHIND THE
CORPORATE FACADE

Q: Do you neglect probing your
corporation's actions for
symbols of a central course
to which it is committed?

A: Usually/Often _____
Sometimes/Seldom _____

ON A GRIM, rainy day a month or so ago, I visited the head-quarters of McDonald's Corporation. My host for this tour was Fred Turner, chairman of the board, and until March 1, 1987, chief executive as well. (On that day, after fourteen years in that job, he turned the reins over to Mike Quinlan.)

We had met at a social gathering where I told him I'd never seen his corporate nerve center in action, and he invited me out. I saw the company's physical plant, noting in particular that executive offices there are open work spaces. No walls. No doors. This is the case for the chairman and president just as much as it is for everyone.

It shouldn't be surprising, then, that Fred Turner doesn't think much of the company's fancy boardroom. As we passed it, such turf normally being a "brag stop" on most of these tours, he bemoaned the fact that a long, awesome table in such a for-mal setting prohibits a meeting where quality communications can take place. "We seldom use it," was his clipped comment to me.

There are many impressive aspects of McDonald's, but what I've chosen to write about was inspired by a small event that took place during that visit. Turner was escorting me through some of the training classes in progress at the renowned Hamburger U. In one, in a test kitchen, he pointed to the trainees working with handheld fire-fighting equipment. He chuckled, turned to me, and said, "Eventually, these people will be tested by being asked to take apart and reassemble this equipment in the dark."

Now, *there's* a symbol!

Rhetoric

Many of us are inclined to look to corporate rhetoric when we want to know a company's course or direction. That's the obvious thing to do, isn't it? Do you seek an answer? Well, then, ask the person who knows and be on your way. The shortest distance between two points is a straight line.

Yet business journalists and investment analysts will tell you crisply that if they relied solely on official corporate rhetoric for ascertaining what a company is ultimately committed to and where it's headed, they'd be the laughing stock of their trade. Their craft demands keeping a gimlet eye turned on corporate pronouncers, no matter how sincerely their pronouncements are uttered.

Actions

Commitment to profits or quality is the official motto of any number of companies. But careful probing of their actions may reveal symbols that show other concerns of more importance. A grandiose Taj Mahal headquarters built by the chief executive as a monument to himself is an example.

The answer to the question should be "sometimes/seldom." Gearing your personal performance goals to a central course in a company such as McDonald's is easier to do than in other companies, because the company's rhetoric and action are more likely to match up. After all, who would argue that precautions for fire safety are anything but documentation of the company's slogan of "quality, cleanliness, service, and value"?

In contrast, there once was a well-known consumer packaged goods company whose chairman and CEO in the 1970s was an upstanding model of civic responsibility and decorum. It's just that he and virtually every member of his top management at headquarters were carrying on affairs. A legitimate spouse at a downtown company reception was a rare sight. That's a symbol too.

Alas, the company and its top management are no more. In the early 1980s it was gobbled up in an acquisition, and most of its pieces were sold off by the buyer. Think those boys weren't paying attention to business?

TAKE ACTION

1. Carefully assess what your company is committed to. Probe what it *does* in opposition to what it says.
2. Sign up or sign out. No company is completely harmonious in word and deed, no matter how well managed. When the divergence is too great, however, signing out is mandatory to avoid cynicism and making you old before your time.

80

TO SEE OURSELVES AS OTHERS SEE US

Q: Do you think you have a good sense of what your associates want from you in your work?

A: Usually/Often _____
Sometimes/Seldom _____

THIS QUESTION IS a little like taking a picture of a photographer taking a picture. Or it's like standing between two mirrors and taking note of your partial images cast off by them.

One of the founders of American sociology was Charles Horton Cooley, who taught at the University of Michigan. Every student in the land in every introductory class in sociology has been made aware of his concept of "the looking-glass self." He captured it poetically by writing, "Each to each a looking glass, the other one doth pass."

The elements of the looking-glass self include (1) how I see myself, (2) how I see the other person I'm in contact with, and (3) how I think he sees me. I have made repeated use of this concept in my consulting work with corporations to show that executives frequently are dealing with partial images in their exchanges with one another.

A photographer who views a picture taken of himself while at work might be in for some surprises, much as most people are the first time they hear their own voice played back to them on a tape recorder.

Executive Development

Whenever I begin an executive development program in a company, meaning a program where executives are coached on how they can improve managing themselves and others, I have them fill out a questionnaire that includes this chapter's question. Now the better answer is, of course, "usually/often," and many of the executives answer the question this way.

However, I also have some of their peers and direct subordinates anonymously fill out the same questionnaire about *them*. I often find that on this question as well as others, the executives' answers are at odds with their associates' responses. In other words, while the executives may think they have a good idea of what their associates want from them, their associates think they do not.

An Attention-Getting Experience

Each executive in the program receives a computer printout that shows how he sees himself—which is a reflection of how he *thinks* his peers, subordinates, and boss see him. But many participants also learn that this picture differs appreciably from how they *really* see him. This is certainly an attention-getting experience!

In a workshop I conduct with a group of executives following their having been through this assessment exercise, they are eager and mobilized to further their skills in, say, listening or setting priorities or decision making, in a way they otherwise would not have been.

There's a lesson here for all of us, and, returning to poetry, it is depicted best in the well-known words of Robert Burns: "Oh wad some power the giftie gie us, To see oursels as others see us!"

TAKE ACTION

1. Don't blithely assume you're picking up all signals from your associates. Ask questions before barging ahead. Make sure what you intend to do in the name of the enterprise is what your associates want and need you to do.
2. Following up on such questions about your contemplated actions, be equally prepared for feedback on what impact your attitudes and bearing have on people. For example, do you talk too much, listen too little? Are you stubborn and dogmatic? Are you tardy to meetings? Do you hog the limelight rather than sharing it with others?

81

AVOIDING
THE TRAPS OF
PROGRESS

Q: **Do you rush to apply the
latest advances in your field
to your work?**

A: Usually/Often _____
Sometimes/Seldom _____

THE DOCTRINE OF inevitable progress is near and dear to the American heart. No problem is so great, we believe, that given enough time and effort, we won't solve it. For example, when we learned in 1986 from the cancer research of Dr. Steven Rosenberg and his team at National Cancer Institute that large doses of interleukin-2 may be a turning point in fighting this killer, we collectively seemed to sigh, "Ah, it was only a matter of time."

A Trendy Distraction?

Belief in inevitable progress shows itself in our dedication to find the better way—to do things more quickly, efficiently, cheaply, beautifully, and so on. In one sense, this is the sum total of industry itself, and each of our jobs is one small link in this chain of events we call progress.

Only a fool chafes at the notion that advancement in technology and method is good and deserves prompt application. Yet I can't forget a former associate of mine who routinely rushed to apply the latest computer and communications technologies to our work, but overslept and missed a critical breakfast meeting with one of our clients.

My experience is that most executives who devote themselves to the latest, best, and state-of-the-art technology are more caught up with novelty, and overlook what is most needed for them. This makes the better answer to the question "sometimes/seldom."

Advancement in Its Time

A great insight came from William F. Ogburn, the University of Chicago sociologist who, in 1922, gave us the concept of cultural lag. His point was that the nonmaterial lags behind the material. Despite today's rhetoric of revolutionary change, Ogburn's thesis holds up. People adapt to material changes on their own time, and cultural change, more accurately, is *evolutionary*.

"Evolutionary" best describes our corporate cultural changes, too. Executives who talk about changing their culture are in for major disappointment if they think this will occur quickly.

So where does all this leave you as an executive bent on making your mark? It leaves you knowing you have to stay abreast of advances in technology and method, but that their application requires discipline about time and place. Panasonic has made hay with its slogan "A step ahead of the times." To the extent that Panasonic is ahead, it's because the company's key decision makers have kept their eyes on the basics and know what the consumer is *now* ready for.

TAKE ACTION

1. Make note of five events over the past three years when you sought to sell your boss on adopting a new method or technology, but failed. Then note whether your proposals were rejected because of cost, because of timing, or because they didn't add significant value. If a rejection was because of cost, learn from that and be prepared in the future to argue more persuasively for what you believe to be the longer-range cost benefits of an idea.
2. If some of your proposals were denied for either of the latter two reasons, face the possibility that you may be inclined to employ mechanisms before their time, or to concentrate on areas that distract you from what your company deems most important. Make a commitment to stop doing this.

82

MAKING THE
EXOTIC MUNDANE

Q: **Are you committed to applying
the obvious, the routine,
the mundane?**

A: Usually/Often _____
    Sometimes/Seldom _____

For a long time I have believed that superior performance, whether from a person or an organization, is dependent on the application of the obvious, the routine, the mundane. Therefore, it comes as no surprise that I consider the better answer to the question to be "usually/often."

Nothing Is More Difficult

When we survey most fields of endeavor, we have very little difficulty coming to agreement about what constitutes superior performance. This is made easy for us by those who set standards—those who, by virtue of their achievements, open a wide gap between themselves and others in the same field.

Whenever we are fortunate enough to observe a champion in action, irrespective of whether the virtuoso performance takes place in athletics, the arts, a business organization, or whatever, we are invariably forced to acknowledge the champion's unerring execution of fundamentals.

Another way of looking at this is to note that what is obviously needed for a head-turning performance is obviously neglected by the bulk of the would-be greats.

Do you want to be an Isaac Stern? Yes? Then be prepared to practice eight hours a day from the age of eight. "Oh, that's a bit too much," you say. Then forget it. There's no other way. But you retort that he's gifted, as Walter Payton is gifted, and what each of them does is natural. I agree, but Stern still practices eight hours a day, and Payton's idea of off-season training during his glorious playing years was to run up a high hill near his house until he threw up. When that happened, he quit for the day.

The Sophisticated Distraction

At the risk of appearing incredibly close-minded—or worse, just plain stupid—I nonetheless would like to offer my view that the reason most organizations leap to adopt the "latest advances" in services (unwittingly, to be sure) is to spare themselves the painful commitment to the basics.

Staying abreast of technology is essential to the growth of any enterprise, but let me repeat from the preceding chapter that the application and usefulness of technology is almost always an evolutionary—rather than revolutionary—process. After all, the electronic computer has been with us over forty years, and we're just now coming around to truly trusting it.

I further think all our current talk about the unprecedented change we face is proof that we have missed the point. First of all, most of this change was foreseen years ago by perceptive executives in all industries. Second, these seers were not listened to by others, who, if they had tried to respond appropriately, would have had to commit themselves afresh to the fundamentals. All the high-tech sophistication and innovation the mind is capable of comprehending cannot spare us the slippage in quality born of poor execution of those innovations and lack of commitment to basic management skills. These are the very basic behavior benchmarks that comprise the subject matter of this book.

In the end, we falter not for failure of nerve in the face of crisis, but for refusing accountability in the face of evolutionary change. Evolutionary change—the real state of affairs—gives us an abundance of time to perfect our crafts. If only we would!

TAKE ACTION

1. Admit that true distinction does not lie in the exotic. It lies in making the seemingly exotic mundane through drill and drudgery.
2. Look around your company once more to reassess who you think the stellar performers are among the numerous executives who rank above you. Be suspicious of those who *talk* about the new era. Rather, get behind those who have delivered the goods year in, year out.

83

A CAUSE FOR UNPOPULARITY

Q: Can you spot flaws in group
decision making when your
subordinates are jointly
grappling with a problem?

A: Usually/Often _____
Sometimes/Seldom _____

THE SEARCH COMMITTEE of the hospital is meeting. This is the session—oh, so long in coming—when the committee will make its decision about which one of the final three candidates will be offered the position of hospital president and chief executive.

All the finalists look good on paper and have particular strengths to offer. All have been interviewed in depth by a sub-committee, and all have been exposed to the full search committee in a general meeting.

An hour passes with various committee members asking questions and making statements about each candidate. It eventually becomes clear that there are two real contenders for the position, with the remaining candidate a distant third.

Another hour passes, and the drift in the committee becomes a rush to the one who is by far the more charismatic of the two. Moreover, the most vocal and dominant member of the committee says he wants to see this candidate on the job because "he's from the Hopper Clinic, and you just can't get better experience than that." It is now 10:00 P.M. The committee members are ready for this day and this search to be over. In effect, they all say aye.

The chairwoman looks around the long conference table and says she has a nagging doubt. Yes, she's read the references on all the candidates and they're fine, but she finds them a little perfunctory—not all that revealing. "Besides," she adds, "Jones is number three at the Hopper Clinic. Good as that place is, he's a lieutenant there, and I'm afraid that's what he'll always be. This job requires a general."

"Now Smith," she continues, "runs St. Louis's Good Shepherd, a much less prestigious medical center, but he runs the whole thing and apparently runs it well. Not only that," she now nods to Dr. Abernathy, the hospital's board chairman, "I think his lower-key personality will make him a better fit with you."

Unpopular Intervention

The search committee as a body is stricken. Exhausted, having worked hard for ten months attending to the broadest issues and minutest details in seeking the finest possible candidate to this first-rate health-care facility, they glare at this woman in full accord for one moment of intense hatred. Then a face here, another there, then still another, softens, and the recognition takes hold among the committee that they do not know all they need to know to reach a firm choice.

Discernment

The chairwoman's discernment was borne out. Despite being drained, the committee members rallied and agreed among themselves to have Jones and Smith interviewed one more time by the subcommittee, and that its membership should now include the chairwoman and Dr. Abernathy. The full committee further agreed to accept whatever hiring decision the subcommittee recommended.

That was twelve years ago. Smith from Good Shepherd in St. Louis got the job and has been superb. Jones from the Hopper Clinic is now number two at a hospital in the Pacific Northwest.

As the chairwoman of this search committee would tell you, the answer to the question should be "usually/often." If you're running something and ultimately bear the burden of its failure, you often have to be the one who upholds high standards.

TAKE ACTION

1. Remember, you're the leader. Resist the temptation to go along with what the group thinks, unless you really believe that the group is right. Look, listen, face up to what you see and hear, swallow hard, and speak up.
2. Be willing to bear any resulting unpopularity. You'll wear well. You'll also set the right example and be a good teacher for those who report to you.

84

THE MYSTERY OF UNINTENDED EFFECTS

Q: **Do you give hard thought to the ways your company *acts* that you and your associates don't understand?**

A: Usually/Often _____
Sometimes/Seldom _____

"I DON'T GET it," the president said. His vice president of administration nodded, munching on his corned beef sandwich. I, the consultant, the third party at this fancy luncheon meeting around the president's desk, merely listened.

The president continued: "For three straight years, we stood our competitors on their ears. The key to our business is new products, a constant flow of them. Some don't make it, of course, but those that do really fly, and the money pours in in buckets. Then, two years ago, things began to come apart. We didn't seem to have as many good ideas, fewer of our products succeeded, and now we're not sitting pretty as we were. We don't know why."

He had more to say: "People around here aren't smiling and as happy as they once were. They're not enjoying their jobs as much. The eroding profits are responsible for that, I guess, but it's also that we're not having success in launching products and seeing them sail. We're all working our tails off, but it's not clicking."

The Apparent

The president of this small company, which manufactures consumer-packaged goods, is an enthusiastic person whose fellowship I enjoy immensely. Moreover, I respect him for the astonishing growth in sales and profits he's brought about in the enterprise since joining it six years ago. He and his management team routinely have outmaneuvered their larger competition in the marketplace.

But the accelerating slippage in the company's market position rightly has him worried. The symptoms of the problem are apparent: failure in generating fresh ideas, loss of market share, and reduced profits. Even the secondary symptoms are easy to spot: harried executives and glum faces. The team is dragging.

A courageous executive, he asks the question: "Is it burnout? My own? The team's?"

I have good news for him: "No."

The Hidden

Dr. Murray Banks, a very funny psychologist, used to say that there is no such thing as a nervous breakdown. Then he would demand: "Show me a nerve that ever broke down!" Similarly, the president and his team in this case have no less capacity than before to create and market new products. But they have less *time*. This is not a marketing problem, but an organizational problem. And it's not one of structure and manpower, but *process*.

The bad news for the president is that his enthusiastic, high-energy, excitement-seeking style is responsible for the current plight. When the company was sluggish, with few new products, his grapeshot, full-speed-forward approach got them launched. Now, with some successful products in tow, his unabating push to keep the pace distracts from the team's efforts both to support current successes and to generate new ones.

The president's motto is "new products," but the way the company acts lets us know that purposes *other* than new products are being served. Those purposes all have to do with the president being too intently "on the case" and working to be at the center of all the important action.

He wants to feel that things are moving. He likes to generate action. He's a practitioner of management by walking around—to a fault. He gets in everybody's hair. He wants to know how everybody's doing—several times a week. He has lots of questions. He has lots of suggestions. And he's right—that the people are working their tails off. But the point is, they could work less and accomplish more. They're too busy responding to this whirling dervish instead of putting their own imagination and knowledge to work.

The president's slower, steady support—directed to fewer successful products rather than his churning on numerous chancy ventures—should turn this company around.

As this company president learned, the answer to the question should be "usually/often."

TAKE ACTION

1. Note some recent puzzling acts of your company. Ponder what purposes these acts served.
2. Ask what priorities took precedence over the intended ones, who set those priorities, and whether *you* can do anything to get things back on track.

85

AN EYE-OPENING IDEA

Q: Do you believe that "form
ever follows function"—that
purpose ultimately determines
structure?

A: Usually/Often _____
Sometimes/Seldom _____

W<small>E ALL KNOW</small> that there can be power in an idea. We know, too, that the more simply it's put, the more clearly it's stated, the more power it has.

Such an idea during World War II was Winston Churchill's telling the English people that he could promise them nothing but blood, toil, tears, and sweat. That thought captured the spirit of the people and rallied an entire nation.

In education, an expression sprang up and became a truism not only for anyone involved in that field, but for those engaged in training and development in the adult world. That expression is: "Repetition is the key to learning."

For our time in American business, such an idea is: "Back to basics."

There is another idea, the subject of this chapter, that has become a part of our language but is not fully comprehended. Written by architect Louis Sullivan in 1896 in *Lippincott's* magazine, it is: "Form ever follows function."

Sullivan died in 1924, broke, a drinker, crushed by the weight of his problems, and totally fallen from the pinnacle of his profession. Yet a genius he was. Frank Lloyd Wright's mentor, he was the father of the graceful skyscraper. His buildings weren't just works of art to the eye; they were marvels of human engineering.

Ever Means Always

By his penetrating statement, now almost a century old, Sullivan didn't mean that architects always designed structures that correctly anticipated their use, but that no matter how it was designed, each structure (that is, form) would undergo change to serve its unshakable *purpose*. This actual use, whether properly foreseen, whether good or bad, whether understood even as it was occurring, is what he meant by "function."

This is an eye-opening idea!

And by "ever" he meant always.

For a moment, think of the CEO of a corporation as its architect. Think of him setting its structure. Keep in mind how complex a corporation is, not only if it's a multinational con-glomerate, but also if it's just a garden-variety manufacturer or service organization with several operating locations and a variety of products and customers.

Think of all its people, each with axes to grind and hav-ing a stake in events. Think of its history, its competitive envi-ronment, its internal culture whose machinations defy easy understanding. Now suppose the CEO, that architect of the cor-poration, gets its function wrong and sets up a dysfunctional structure.

Not According to Plan

It happens all the time. Whenever we hear the expression "Things didn't go according to plan," we may be sure somebody made the wrong call on function. This is why the answer to the question should be "usually/often." Any architect who thought he was designing a community's cultural arts facility but then saw it spurned and later converted to a senior citizens' center knows the meaning of misinterpreting the true function of a structure.

For a generation the Japanese have clobbered us with their seven levels of corporate management. We've stood by, losing ground, with fifteen or so. Again, we may be sure that functions and purposes other than business competitiveness were at play. Form *ever* follows function.

But now, thank you, a healthier function is taking hold and it's symbolized in the powerful idea of the day: "Back to basics." Look out, Japan.

TAKE ACTION

1. Believe that form ever follows function, not vice versa. Sullivan's legacy is one that can have profound impact on our understanding of corporate cultures.

2. If you see a gap between anticipated function and actual function in your organization, speak up. The CEO or any boss can't know it all. The corporation is incredibly complex. Give your ideas. Management today is more than ever a collaborative process, and your contribution to the team is needed.

86

DESIRE:
THE FUEL FOR
FORTITUDE

Q: **Do you avoid naming true desires in your life, your company, your projects?**

A: Usually/Often _____
Sometimes/Seldom _____

W E TEND TO avoid naming desires in our lives for at least a couple of reasons. One of them is that the word sounds selfish. It violates our typical view of responsibility, which implies our obligations to others. Yet there is another sense of responsibility—to ourselves—which requires that we be who we really are and believe in what we do. For unless we believe in what we're doing, it's hard to excel at it, and even harder to be happy at it. This should lead us to answer the question "sometimes/seldom."

Wishes and Desires

We all have wishes. They are the "Wouldn't it be nice?" element of living. Social psychologist W. I. Thomas held that all people have four broad wishes: (1) recognition, (2) love, (3) new experiences, and (4) security. When we examine these, we readily agree, "Yes, wouldn't they be nice?" Yet what are we willing to do to make sure each is characteristic of our lives? Excuse the pun, but less than we would wish for.

We are easily discouraged from our wishes. For example, sailing is something I wish I did. However, my wish evaporates whenever I consider the seemingly endless labors to be attended to before a boat can leave its mooring. In addition, I contemplate the preparation and maintenance of the boat to make and keep it waterworthy. Last, I mull over the most formidable item of all: learning to sail.

For me, these labors make sailing an unpalatable undertaking. On the other hand, for many of my friends—whom I envy—these are labors of love. For them, sailing is not a wish, but a desire. They recognize the work involved for what it is, but their desire sees them through.

Refining Our Gifts

A second reason we avoid naming our desires in both our personal and work lives ties in with my opening comments about responsibilities to ourselves. These are responsibilities that involve facing up to labors of love—labors that bring us joy and exhilaration ultimately, but in the interim, occasionally pain and suffering.

The late Dorothy Parker, one of our first-rate writers, once remarked: "I hate writing, but I love having written." I resonate with that. When I named sailing, I discovered that I was dealing with a wish, not a desire. But a few years ago, when I named writing, I named a desire. Sometimes I dread writing these chapters, but I always take pleasure in having written them. Nobody makes me do it, and I look forward to mastering it.

Confronting desire squarely is to acknowledge what we owe ourselves, and that we're going to take a run at something costing us toil and anguish. It is to know failure, but to overcome it in giving to those around us what is most distinctive about our lives. That's the paradoxical payoff. By refining our gifts, we meet the responsibility to ourselves that also meets our responsibility to others.

TAKE ACTION

1. Write down fifteen accomplishments you would like to make yours. Include some from on and off your job. Review that list carefully. Draw a line through those you conclude are wishes rather than desires.
2. Think hard about the remaining few items. By doing so, you're likely to discover what gifts you have that need refining. Get on with it. Your desire will see you through.

87

WISHING WON'T MAKE IT HAPPEN

Q: Do you distinguish between
wishes and desires?

A: Usually/Often ‗‗‗‗‗
Sometimes/Seldom ‗‗‗‗‗

THERE ARE VARIOUS mental images we all entertain frequently that represent life to us not as it is, but as we'd like it to be. Two of them that deserve understanding because of their impact on our job performance are wishes and desires.

Wishes

I had boarded the DC-10 in Los Angeles. It was bound for Chicago. As I closed the overhead bin after storing my briefcase, I looked around the cabin before sitting down. A few rows back, occupying a window seat on the left side of the airplane, was Barbara Eden.

I've never been much of a TV watcher, but I'm pretty good at remembering names and faces. And on a couple of occasions I caught snatches of a sitcom she starred in over a decade ago. Do you remember its name? It shouldn't be too difficult because it's been in reruns for years. It was *I Dream of Jeannie*.

The male star of the show was none other than Larry Hagman—today's reprobate J. R. Ewing on *Dallas*—but here he played a sort of nice, inept type who needed bailing out of his foolishness regularly. "Jeannie" was of course a takeoff on "genie," and beautiful Barbara was available to laughable Larry with all sorts of loving advice and miracles at the snap of his fingers. This idle bumbler kept getting himself into jams and could extricate himself only with the magical intervention of his resident rescuer. Without his wishes being granted, his vapid existence would have sunk even lower.

Desires

Desire is a mental image entirely different from wish and potentially far more powerful. Whereas wish entails idleness (Larry Hagman's role of helplessness was perfect for conveying this), desire is more likely to lead to action and resourcefulness.

In the last chapter, I wrote that I wished I knew how to sail. My point was that this meant I never would take up sailing. On the other hand, if I'm able to identify desire in my life, therein lies the fuel for fortitude, to make something happen that I'm already committed to.

Elizabeth, an older woman in Mary Gordon's novel *The Company of Women*, ruminates about her lifelong faith:

> Still, I make prayers of petition because I believe one good comes of it: the expression of desire. It is good to know what one longs for, and to know it clearly; in the area of desire, one should not err.

This wise woman knows that to ignore desire, or accommodate it poorly, is to invite mischief into our lives. In other words, desire is destiny, for good or ill. The answer to the question, then, should be "usually/often."

We link our sense of responsibility on the job most often to what we owe others. There's nothing wrong with this joint tenancy in our minds except that it obscures the remaining responsibility we have to ourselves. This responsibility is the most difficult we face because it entails our taking a run at what we long for most deeply, and it sometimes causes us pain before we experience its pleasure. Honesty about what we truly desire to accomplish and all we have to do to bring it about, however, is essential if we are to excel.

Such desire is spawned early in us and never departs, though we often do our best to ignore or subvert it and, as this older woman implies, this is folly. Accommodating desire is the only hope for bringing us more fully into harmony with ourselves, and it is what leads to distinctive, exhilarating performance in our work.

Imagine putting Elizabeth's remarkable insight to work on our jobs! Imagine our initiative when we realize that responsibility to our associates in our companies means, in the last analysis, that we are responsible to ourselves. That is, we take action on what we are already committed to inside. This kind of commitment is what sustains us when failure threatens, and leads to final performance that wins the admiration and appreciation of subordinates, peers, and higher management alike.

TAKE ACTION

1. Sit back for half an hour and let honest answers come to you about what is—or should be—happening in your area of responsibility that you're committed to emotionally, but that you have somehow overlooked or ignored.
2. Lay your mere wishes aside and give yourself over to this ready-made commitment. This is the stuff of achievers.

88

WORKING THROUGH PAIN

Q: **Do you run from adversity?**

A: Usually/Often ———
Sometimes/Seldom ———

A FEW MONTHS ago, I was asked by the vice president of administration of a well-known company in the Southwest to do a consulting assignment. It may sound like an unusual one to some readers, but it is the kind of task I've gotten involved in frequently.

My assignment was to help restore a faltering relationship between this multinational company's CEO and the president of its domestic businesses. These two executives had worked together for years and knew each other well—or so they thought.

Most such assignments require getting past some discomforting moments of self-consciousness and embarrassment between the two parties, but they usually turn out well. What is required is that I first spend a few hours with each person separately. I have both people describe their jobs, career histories, working relationship with each other, and problems with that relationship as they see it.

Second, I assemble them in a room off-site for a day where I serve as a facilitator. My job is mainly to develop empathy— to have each one become aware of the other's point of view. In the process of doing this, distortions that have been built up over a period of months (sometimes years) have a way of disappearing. Each begins to see ways that he has adopted to act in response to these phantoms. Such distortions, of course, further aggravate the situation and generate heat rather than light.

Seeing how their lack of interpersonal communication has led to joint misunderstanding of each other's motives and actions, mature executives are usually quick to find and implement remedies.

This Time a Failure

In this case, however, it's doubtful that I succeeded. In meetings with the CEO and the domestic president, they both expressed relief that the problem between them was being addressed.

They also both agreed to a joint meeting off the premises, and said they would be back in touch with me to schedule it.

Letting two or three weeks go by between the initial one-on-one meetings and the joint one can provide a good gestation period for this kind of process. But when a month elapsed with no word from the client, I called the vice president of administration. He told me that the two executives thought the exercise had already accomplished its purpose, and they had reached an agreement on how they could better work together in the future.

Choosing Expedience

Now, in fact, there may be reasons other than "misunderstanding" that have led to one or both of these executives not truly resolving their differences. For example, the domestic president may simply want the CEO's job; he may be trying to keep the rivalry alive and put the best possible face on it. The CEO may be aware of this; he in turn may be determined to squeeze the president out while keeping his own hands clean.

But I don't think that's true in this case. Rather, I think this is an occasion when two people chose expedience and talked themselves out of the hard adversity and embarrassment of going head-to-head to achieve full clarity. And it is a reminder that as executives we can never refine our gifts—most of them intangible—unless we're willing to work our way through periodic pain of one kind or another.

I hope that you, unlike these two executives, won't run from adversity and can answer the question "sometimes/seldom."

TAKE ACTION

1. Don't shirk adversity. No pain, no gain. Whatever adversity you face, chances are that it won't go away just because you do. It is likely to continue to haunt you.

2. Think about adversity you have run from, but now realize has remained your shadow. Stop looking over your shoulder. Turn around. Face it. After you deal with the adversity, you'll be amazed at how much energy it had been sapping that you can now put to constructive use somewhere else.

89

THE GIFTS THAT ARE YOU

Q: Do you think of yourself as gifted?

A: Usually/Often _____
Sometimes/Seldom _____

SITTING ABOARD PSA'S Flight 1721 from Los Angeles to San Francisco, where I'll attend a meeting, I realize I need something better to do than get irritated by the slob to my left. This coarse fellow tears the top off his bag of honey-roasted peanuts and throws it on the floor. He grabs the airline magazine from the seat pocket in front of him and turns the pages while he loudly chomps on his peanuts. Twice he comes to a page containing an insert card that falls out into his lap, and he throws it on the floor. When he finishes his peanuts, he crumples up the bag and throws that on the floor too. He's done all this in the space of five minutes. He's a study in motion.

The Guru

Impulsively, I reach for *my* copy of the magazine. "Ah, saved!" I say to myself. "Now I can get my mind on something more constructive." On the cover is a professor of marketing at Stanford's graduate school of business. He's Michael Ray, viewed in these parts as a guru on creativity in business. He's the subject of an interview.

I read the interview, nodding in agreement with all but one of Ray's points, and place the magazine back into the seat pocket, pondering some of them. Then I find my thoughts going to that one notion of his I find troublesome. It's one we hear often that says to be creative, you mustn't struggle. Drudgery brings only misery, not ideas or solutions. Creativity flows only from the mind at play. No argument there, I conclude. I buy the latter part, but am quick to caution that sometimes it is drudgery and drill that bring the mind to the playground.

Resourcefulness, Not Creativity

Where Ray and I would agree totally is that what we call creativity is a set of gifts we all have. Common confusion about what creativity is and who can have it can be traced to the word itself. As with "leadership" or "vision," "creativity" has lost its meaning. It means whatever the user wants it to mean. If you're a person who thinks you're not creative, as many do, let me suggest that you replace that word with "resourcefulness." I say this because creativity in fact is nothing more or less than making full use of your personal resources, making use of your *gifts*. And more often than not, making use of your gifts involves hard work and taking risks that others avoid. This is something I described in Chapter 87 when dealing with the subject of desire.

Even this slob to my left, bubbling with energy, is loaded with gifts. Although he is lacking in manners, a trait that is bound to offend others as well as me, and therefore likely to limit his effectiveness, I can see that he has much to offer any enterprise. I wonder, for example, if all his agitated activity is akin to a thoroughbred stamping at the gate before the bell rings and then set free to run as no other. I don't know, of course, but it would make a fascinating subject of discussion were we to get to know each other.

Resourceful people don't waste time and effort wishing for gifts they don't have, but are grateful for and use the ones they've got. Executives who do distinctive things see gifts not as entities exotic and rare and beyond their grasp—such as "creativity"—but as possessions of their own they seek to lay hold of. For them, the answer to the question is "usually/often."

TAKE ACTION

1. Many executives produce mediocre results because they see themselves as commodities, like grain or pork bellies. See yourself as the gifts you have.
2. Since you're gifted, get serious about the actions that will bring you to the playground. What is it about yourself that you truly like? What do you have to do to put that into play in the best possible way? Now's the time to get started.

90

BEATING THE BLIPS

Q: **Do you have difficulty picking yourself up after a "fair and square" loss in business?**

A: Usually/Often _____
     Sometimes/Seldom _____

TODAY I'M THINKING about:

- The advertising agency that goes full speed ahead; burns the midnight oil, with its account and creative team members laughing, crying, and fighting with one another during several stress-filled weeks; prepares a campaign and presentation to win a prized account—only to lose out to a competitor who seems somehow to be able to offer more of what the client wants.
- The product development and marketing teams in a pharmaceuticals company whose members painstakingly develop new compounds; test, retest, and test some more; gain FDA approval; and, after exhaustive market research, name the product and package it attractively; celebrate their endurance over the eight years it takes to do all this by bringing the product to market—and then see it flop.
- The executive who has convinced his boss over a period of eighteen months that their business has come to a fork in the road, and who argues that the business should go left, but the boss accepts the recommendation of one of the executive's peers that it go right, hands *him* the baton, and leaves our early hero empty-handed.
- Anyone and everyone who labors long and loses.

Fair and Square

The examples of failure I've given are those that are clean; no foul play is present, just honest effort that didn't produce the desired effect. It happens all the time.

What is present in all these examples, however, is the element of competition, even in the case of the pharmaceutical that flopped. While it may not have had a direct competitor, it was not perceived as offering enough value-added to buyers who felt that existing products of one kind or another met their needs. Soft-drink makers, for instance, will tell you that plain water is one of their competitors.

There are all kinds of reasons why we lose when we're up against formidable competition, and they're too numerous to mention here. There is always the possibility, for example, that we haven't listened well, haven't done our homework before our efforts at delivery, and have just missed the point. The competition, having avoided those mistakes, then waltzes in.

But I'm more concerned in this chapter with those times when you seem to have gotten it all together, are proud of your efforts, wouldn't change what you did, but *still* come out second best.

The Long View

Most often, there just isn't an answer to this predicament that gives us any immediate satisfaction. The only image I've found helpful in such cases is the marathon and remembering that the real race doesn't begin until the twenty-third mile. Work and life have to be nurtured over the long haul. *Tenacity, then, is the key.* Tenacity is what's called for when we're smart enough to take the long view or confused enough to have lost it. This is the kind of mind-set necessary for overcoming periodic, inevitable losses.

When you lose in a competitive business situation, you are not alone in your bafflement. All of us have trouble figuring out why we lose and the other person or group wins. Yet, I promise you, this kind of confusion will sort itself out eventually if you'll pick yourself up and keep on pursuing what you've committed yourself to.

The long view will ultimately serve you well. It will spare you from the erosion of self-esteem that is brought about when you fail and are inclined to feel that you are without gifts, or have lost the ones you had. Trust your long-term commitment to your professional values and goals, and they will spur you afresh to reclaim and refine the gifts you have. This attitude will enable you to answer the question "sometimes/seldom."

TAKE ACTION

1. Don't deny your discouragement. It's real and under-standable. Own it. That way it won't go underground and own you without your knowing it. Then you'll be able to get up and get moving again.
2. Great companies have strategies that are sacrosanct. They stick with them despite the blips. So do great people. Imitate them.

91

MAKING MEETINGS WORK

Q: Do you see yourself as a willing participant in a collaborative management process?

A: Usually/Often _____
Sometimes/Seldom _____

Executives complain about meetings the way everybody complains about the weather, with about the same results. Despite the fact that meetings, unlike weather, are a creation of mankind, we seem no less under their control than we are subject to the decrees of Mother Nature. We complain, but we wouldn't dare do without. The meeting has a purpose that cannot be denied.

A Demand for Collaboration

We live at a time when we have to believe that two or more heads are better than one and authoritarianism is bad form. Both the state of mind and rule of practice emerged in our dim anticipation that the process of evolutionary change is going to demand much of each of us if we're going to adapt well to life on and around this planet.

All this sounds a bit grand when what concerns us is that meetings claim a disproportionate share of our time and keep us from getting our work done. But this view displays a misunderstanding of what "work" today means for the executive. Most probably this view is also a reflection of poor management of his time.

Part of the misunderstanding of work stems from the fact that, believe it or not, thinking is not considered work while *motion* is. Thinking is something we have to get out of the way before we can get to work. Yet down deep, we realize it will take the best output of all our minds to meet the challenges of the future. This is why the meeting not only persists, but grows in importance. It's a forum that forces us to think.

Are You a Willing Participant?

Much of our impatience with meetings stems from giving so much time to something before it produces value. No wonder we complain and are unwilling participants in this process! But do we ask what prepared thoughts we're bringing to the meeting that make that meeting valuable to our associates? Not usually, nor do they, with the result that fruitful meetings are accidents.

In no way am I a critic of brainstorming. I endorse it enthusiastically. But brainstorming should be used sparingly, only after solo preparation for the session by each participant.

True collaboration—the ideal of most meetings—takes place when all participants give voice to their ideas based on "thinking assignments" given in advance. Those assignments may be given by the chairperson in some cases, or by the work group itself at the conclusion of a prior meeting.

Various participants should be asked to think hard about defining or redefining problems, options, alternatives, and consequences; evaluating past performance; and so on. This is real work, which is why many of us shun it. But it eliminates our coming to meetings where most of us talk off the top of our heads and waste valuable time in "group grope." For this reason, your answer to the question should be "usually/often."

TAKE ACTION

1. Give serious thought to the meetings you call for yourself and your subordinates. Get hard-nosed with yourself about what you want from each gathering. Make sure each participant knows that his job is to produce *ideas*.
2. Suggest the same process for meetings you attend with your peers and boss. You'll be amazed at your quickened achievements, personally and in concert.

92

SPEAR CARRIER
IN COMMITTEE

Q: **Do you resent the increasing predominance of collaborative give-and-take prior to decision making?**

A: Usually/Often _____
   Sometimes/Seldom _____

On MAY 16, 1949, a giant in his field sent the following memo to all his staff:

> I have just realized what it is that Americans do when they would rather not do anything—about something.
> They form a committee.
> A committee is a group of three or more men and women who manage to take from three weeks to three years to do what one person could do in half an hour of either concentration or good hard work.
> A committee is a device to put off indefinitely the making of a decision.
> It is a shield behind which to retreat, hoping that somehow the retreat will become an advance—with somebody else carrying the spear.

The giant in this case was the late Fairfax Cone, the dominant force for almost thirty years at Foote, Cone & Belding, the standard-setting advertising firm. David Ogilvy said of him: "The ad-game is not without its statesmen and Fairfax Cone is the most admirable of them."

Individual Initiative

Were the insightful Fairfax Cone alive today, I'd bet a week's pay he'd say he called this one wrong forty years ago. And while the resentment he expressed for what we now could call collaborative give-and-take is still around, it's a fire largely extinguished. For this reason, the answer to the question should be "sometimes/seldom."

One of the main points in the griping about collaborative management is that it destroys individual initiative. How so? True enough, it has put a collar around authoritarian types who were accustomed to cutting a wide swath through their organizations while barking out orders carried out by dutiful minions.

Yet collaboration before decision making has opened up possibilities for many more to take initiative by way of their *ideas.* Any ad hoc, temporary work group, project team, or task force today under the direction of an able facilitator is likely to be staffed almost totally with high-spirited contributors.

It is undeniably true that reaching a group-generated decision will take longer than when a solitary person decides while keeping his own counsel. But chances are great that the decision made after collaboration will lead to more efficient performance in the long run. This is partly because most people are more likely to cooperate with a decision wholeheartedly if they had some say in it.

Convene, Join, or Shun?

The central issue for you, assuming you're bent on taking initiative, is knowing which ad hoc group to be a part of. Join only those whose leaders have a record of facilitating collaboration and have shown the will to make bold decisions. If you believe in a task that isn't getting done, and believe this is the time for it, then perhaps *you* should convene the group and be its leader.

Remember, collaboration is not for making decisions, but for defining problems and generating options *prior* to making decisions. Sometimes consensus develops, and that's nice. But it's more important to remember that true, quality decision making is choosing, from all the competing options presented through collaboration, the *one* that will lead to distinctive results. Usually that choice falls to the person sitting at the end of the table.

TAKE ACTION

1. Commit yourself to the notion that your initial contribution in committee action is to use your brain to generate

your share of alternatives and have the courage to argue for them.

2. Accept that your brain and voice won't always prevail. Others will prove more insightful and persuasive than you on occasion. But speak up anyway. You'll find that people will pay attention to you, and a fair share of decisions will go your way.

93

FACING THE
RIGHT DEMANDS

Q: **Do you think your job fails
to make the right demands
on you?**

A: Usually/Often _____
Sometimes/Seldom _____

IT'S COMMON FOR us to use animal imagery when describing corporations and their businesses. Many of these references are favorable, such as when we label a market leader the "lion of the industry," or speak of a company known for its strong sales, distribution, and service coverage as having "ants all over the hill."

Other descriptions are, of course, negative. An example of this is when we call a company that hasn't kept up with the times a "lumbering old elephant" or "dinosaur." Another is when we speak of a company as "ostrich-like," burying its head in the sand.

Animal analogies for executives themselves are apt as well, and here, too, they're not all favorable. One in particular struck me moments ago as I recalled seeing a small piece of tacky statuary in an Ogunquit, Maine, tourist shop a few summers ago. I didn't buy it, but have it pictured in my mind as if it were sitting in front of me.

The little statue was of three sitting monkeys. The first sees no evil, the second hears no evil, and the third speaks it not. But the subject that is prompted for me by these creatures isn't evil but opportunity. The three little monkeys remind me of executives who see no opportunity, hear no opportunity, and won't speak of it.

Peripheral Vision

Do you remember the last time you were in a restaurant and needed to get your server's attention, but couldn't? After the entrées were placed down, you noticed that the sauce your guest asked for on the side was not brought at all. Or you wanted another glass of wine—now—not when your meal was finished. Or you were in a hurry and just wanted the check.

What makes this situation especially annoying is that your server is scurrying all around you, but for some reason you can't catch his eye with your own or an unobtrusive gesture. (Try leaving without paying the bill, however!)

You're annoyed because the server chooses not to make use of his peripheral vision. The server doesn't *want* your eyes to meet. Something will be requested by you, and for reasons of busyness or laziness, such requests are loathsome.

Eyes, Ears, and Mouth

Many executives are just like this incompetent server, except that their poor performance is not limited to their self-imposed blinders. They also refuse to take the responsibility for hearing what's needed from them by their associates, or for speaking up when they should be persuasive on some issue.

Ironically, I've found that executives marked by such behavior, and whose financial rewards for their work match the pattern of tips paid to the server whose attention cannot be won, are those who think their jobs are boring. They claim that their jobs fail to make enough of the right demands on them. They convince us—to their surprise—that the answer to the question should be "sometimes/seldom."

All of us can remember teachers or professors we had along the way who answered questions nobody was asking. They remind me of the executives I've been describing—bent on providing what nobody is asking for, while through gyrating and misspent activity, they fail to provide what is needed. They may claim to be bored, but they have not given enough thought to three questions their companies are asking: (1) Do you know what we want to have done? (2) Where will superior work by you produce maximum impact? and (3) How will you make use of your gifts to do superior work?

In earlier chapters, I've urged you to discover what you believe in and make sure you act on it in your work. This may have prompted an exasperated question of your own: "Is Cox crazy? I'm so busy doing what my bosses are asking that I've got no time left for my druthers!"

If you have felt this, these three questions of mine may help clarify the confusion. You won't be able to perform with distinction if your heart isn't in it. But you must make the time in quiet moments off the job to think hard and be imaginative in finding ways that put your gifts and values into play on what your company wants done. Do this right and people will stay out of your way! They'll want you to do what you do best. The ball is in your court.

TAKE ACTION

1. I know it's a cliché, but it's still good advice: See problems—some of them, anyway—as opportunities. Wrap your gifts around them.
2. Speak up! Go recruit people in your company who can help you undertake and excel in some risky but worthwhile project. Don't try to carry the whole load yourself. Although the company wants it done, others may be afraid to try. This will be a feather in your cap.

94

TAPPING UNLIKELY RESOURCES

Q: Do you observe the abilities
and interests of a wide range
of people in your entire
company, with an eye to how
they might join you on some
project?

A: Usually/Often _____
Sometimes/Seldom _____

LATE WEDNESDAY AFTERNOON, February 12, 1986, the CEO of an Eastern Coast pharmaceuticals company convened a hastily assembled task force. He called the meeting so that he and his associates could think through ways to avert a crisis.

Earlier in the week, Johnson & Johnson had had its second terrifying instance of some deranged person lacing its Tylenol product with cyanide, causing death to an unsuspecting taker. The CEO and everyone in the room realized the urgency of the situation and sought ways to prevent the same problem from occurring with any of their own products. Moreover, the CEO admired the way J&J executives had handled their first crisis. His hope was that he and his executives could do as well if it came to that.

Round and round they went, discussing protective packaging changes they might make, whether they should convert their product to caplets, or even whether they might temporarily pull their products from drugstore and grocery-chain shelves or stop making them altogether. These and all conceivable alternatives were considered.

At one point, however, the CEO wheeled around in his chair and spoke courteously but pointedly to the newest member of the management team who was present at the meeting: "Steve, we've been at it for almost an hour, and you haven't said a word. C'mon, guy, you think we asked you here because you're an expert in taxes?"

Beyond Labels

Now, the fact of the matter is that Steve *had* been hired six months earlier by this company because he *was* an expert in taxes. But he was also much more than that, and those added dimensions are what led to his being selected for his job as vice president of taxes over several other candidates, including one from inside the company.

The chief financial officer who hired him saw imagination, poise, and breadth in him—qualities that are often lacking in tax specialists. The CFO had had his beliefs about Steve confirmed in the few months he had worked with him so far, and had even begun to think of him as someone he could groom as a potential successor to himself. He had conveyed his enthusiasm to the CEO, and the CEO had concurred, on the basis of his brief exposure to Steve. That's why he thought it would be good to have Steve's contribution at this meeting. He got it, too, just by asking, by not letting him be timid, even though he was the new kid on the block.

Beyond Departments

Following the lead of the CEO, we know that the answer to the question should be "usually/often."

Some people think they must follow a strict chain of command in giving and getting information and securing other help in their projects. Not so. In my book *Inside Corporate America*, a study of 1,086 top and middle executives in thirteen major corporations, nine out of ten from both levels indicate that they always or usually are free to exchange resources with people in other departments without approval from their bosses.

Do you remember my story about Gary Dillon in Chapter 59? Remember how this CEO of Household Manufacturing built this company by empowering others, by making them stretch, by getting them to do more than they thought they could do? Remember how he inspired them with the expression, "We have found the edge and it is us"? Gary looks beyond labels and beyond departments to get things done.

We all need to think this way.

TAKE ACTION

1. Approach your everyday job with a task-force mentality. Realize that resourceful, concerned people bring gifts beyond their job titles.
2. Be a facilitator, a catalyst of these resources. Don't wait for someone else to do what needs to be done. Do it yourself. Be like the CEO in this situation. Ask.

95

DON'T HESITATE, FACILITATE!

Q: Do you make it clear to others in your company that you are available to help them on projects they undertake?

A: Usually/Often _____
Sometimes/Seldom _____

I'M ALWAYS FASCINATED with how certain expressions come onto the scene for a while and give vent to how we're feeling. Some fade rather quickly, but others hang on, indicating a more persistent attitude abroad in the land.

One that comes to mind that's proved its durability over the past few years is "Have a good one." As we know, this has become a common send-off between one party and another, such well-wishing being applied to an endless variety of time periods and events. This good-natured support is appreciated and met with a "Thanks," and, if appropriate, also reciprocated. "You too," says the beneficiary.

Thinking of reciprocating also brings to mind another expression that came into popular usage a few years ago and has held firm. It's "I owe you one." These often repeated words and their derivatives, such as Lee Iacocca's saying "We owe 'em one" in reference to the Carter administration's bailout of Chrysler Corporation, reinforce the notion that one good turn deserves another.

Giving First

Aside from the getters and takers who seem to believe there *is* such a thing as a free lunch as long as it's for them, most of us are pretty good at returning favors. If others go out of their way for us, we're usually prompt at saying thank you at least, or paying tribute in more significant ways.

This repayment on our part is as it should be, and we're pleased to make it. But we must admit that the help given on our behalf ordinarily has come as a surprise. We didn't expect it. We thought our associates were so absorbed with their own concerns and projects that they had little or no time for ours.

Or, simply to reverse that, knowing how taken we are with our own tasks, with little time or energy left over to give to others, how could we expect anything but the same from them?

Just imagine, then, the impact on your associates if you would convert the "I owe you one" from the reactive to the proactive mode. Imagine the pleasant surprises all around and the people in *your* debt because you make clear to them—and prove it with your actions—that you're available and eager to help them out.

The answer to the question should be "usually/often."

An Old Expression

An expression that's been around all my life, and probably predates it, is "If you want to get something done, give it to a busy person."

You're ahead of me, I'm sure. My point here, simply, is that we can handle infinitely more than we think we can. I'm urging you to be that person who volunteers his help to surprised and grateful coworkers.

TAKE ACTION

1. Don't think about how much work you have to do. Instead, think about making a *contribution*. Ask or suggest how you can lend a helping hand.
2. Don't wait, hesitate, procrastinate. Facilitate! You'll be amazed at both how much help you get in kind and the quality and quantity of your joint accomplishments.

96

A SOFT RESIDUAL

Q: Do you dismiss intuition as a
"soft" subject and avoid
listening to your inner voice
when making decisions?

A: Usually/Often _____
Sometimes/Seldom _____

Not LONG AGO, *Business Week*'s star management editor John Byrne wrote up an interview he conducted with the amazing, near-octogenarian Peter Drucker at the latter's Rocky Mountain retreat in Colorado.

Near the end of the interview, Byrne asked Drucker whether he thought American managers had become too taken with "soft" disciplines in carrying out their responsibilities. As an example, Byrne made reference to the well-received book *The Intuitive Manager* by Roy Rowan.

Drucker was in fine form and good humor. He said things had gone too soft partially because the legion of parasites (consultants) like him were out peddling their wares, feeding off the system.

Then he got more serious and said that he had been around for fifty years and observed that business is forever susceptible to fads, with one cycle following another. He said that recently, we've had corporate culture (a soft idea) followed by ethics (a very soft idea). He then predicted that next we'll have a hard idea come into vogue, followed by a very hard one. He gives the soft stuff "eighteen months" and points to advances in accounting techniques.

The Spiral Theory

I have no reason to doubt Drucker's prediction. Like most other members of the business community, I'm in awe of his command of a wide range of subjects, his powers of mind—which seem undiminished with age—and his perception about the meaning of events.

Yet when that next hard cycle comes around, it will merely be in the foreground, with the soft stuff simply receding to the background. I don't believe it will disappear.

I have always been taken with the eighteenth-century Italian social philosopher Giovanni Vico, developer of the spiral theory. He asserted that society is not strictly cyclical, that it does not return to itself, but that when a given cycle is completed it finds itself on a higher plane than when that cycle began.

All such cycles within the spiral evolutionary movement have their constructive and corrective elements. The corporate culture phenomenon, the enormous acceptance of *In Search of Excellence* by Thomas Peters and Robert Waterman, and the emergent concern for ethics are all powerful expressions that the human factor was being neglected in corporate management and decision making. If we've now gone overboard in this way, let the hard stuff come and we'll all be better off.

Intuition's Antiquity

Having enjoyed a resurgence of attention, intuition is a little like the color yellow having been mixed with a second one to produce a third. It lost its outward identity for a time, but not its power. Then along comes someone who says, "I'd like to see something in yellow" and it is brought out again.

So the hard stuff won't supplant the soft stuff, especially something like intuition that has shown its durability over the entire history of man. Advances in accounting and information systems will inexorably present themselves on the management landscape—God bless them, we need them—but listening to your inner voice is necessary when all the information you ever wanted isn't enough. The answer to the question should be "sometimes/seldom."

TAKE ACTION

1. If in doubt, don't make another pass at the facts and figures, but look *inside* instead.
2. Look deeper. Is the doubt really genuine doubt, or just plain fear? If the latter, make this the occasion when you finally subdue this demon and learn the joy and result of trusting your gut.

97

VISION: NOT CLAIRVOYANCE, BUT UNDERSTANDING

Q: **Do you believe vision is a collaborative undertaking?**

A: Usually/Often _____
Sometimes/Seldom _____

Over the last few years, *Business Week* has run a feature every twelve months in which it announces what's "in" and what's "out" in the current year.

If you haven't seen the *Business Week* feature, you've probably seen the same kind of thing in other places. It strikes most people as good reading entertainment. I think it gets our attention because, while we might not want to bet our last dollar on some of its predictions, we usually find them intriguing. In any event, we are certainly in a better position to consider their plausibility than to dispute them.

One of *Business Week*'s predicted "outs" in 1988 is rock music. The "in" music taking its place is country and western. And darned if I haven't been hearing more stations playing that wailing sound lately. Not only that, just listen to Bruce Springsteen's recent album *Tunnel of Love*, and you'll hear plenty of twang. See what I mean?

So I found it particularly fascinating that *Business Week* pronounced *strategy* "out" and *vision* "in." I think its predictors are right on the mark.

False Starts and Failed Strategies

In my 1985 book *The Making of the Achiever*, I wrote:

> I am not one to glamorize the management practices of the Japanese. I believe that has been overdone, and that before long the Japanese will again have much to learn from us. However, there is one area of their business practice that I find admirable. Predictably enough, it is one we Americans chide them for. That practice is for the upper echelons of their corporate management seemingly to talk a subject to death before reaching a decision on it.
>
> What the Japanese method (that we find so inefficient) produces is quality *communication*. It generates an inquiring disposition and fertile, inclusive thought. And what it eliminates are inappropriate goals and false starts. We Americans are known by our false starts and changed courses. While the Japanese are slow to reach decisions, their decisions are more "true" than ours with the result that their *execution* is more efficient than ours.

Vision as Understanding

The success of the Japanese shows that the answer to the question should be "sometimes/seldom." The reason, however, that I think Japan won't be able to maintain its superiority over us in production quality and service is that we are a far more resourceful country overall and are adopting Japan's predominant management method.

That method is the exercise of vision. Most Americans erroneously have thought of vision as an attempt at distant clairvoyance. In other words, a high-stakes guessing game. The Japanese, on the other hand, take vision to mean understanding. And they know that understanding can't come without engaging the minds of their executives in serious, disciplined, time-consuming debate. This is necessary for reaching conclusions on where their companies are and where they're headed. Then and only then are they in a position to decide to stay on course or change it. Then and only then are they in a position to choose—and commit themselves to—a mission and goals that point far into the future.

TAKE ACTION

1. See corporate strategy for what it is: the second step. Vision comes first and tells management "where." It answers the questions "Where are we as a company? Where are we headed? Is this good?" This is best achieved by much discussion before final conclusions are drawn.
2. Devise strategy based on "what." Now that we know where we're headed, what do we have to do to keep things going this way, if we believe our direction is good? Or, what do we do if our direction is leading us astray from our mission and we need to stop in our tracks? Then devise tactics based on "how." How do we do it?

98

TYRANTS
NEED NOT APPLY

Q: Are your subordinates hesitant
to initiate activities and projects without your instigation?

A: Usually/Often _____
Sometimes/Seldom _____

YESTERDAY I WAS in Phoenix to address the annual management meeting of The Sherwin-Williams Company. There, about one hundred key executives plus their spouses or partners were gathered over a three-day period to review plans for the coming fiscal year.

It's a nifty idea—and unusual—to include spouses in these meetings. Although their attendance is optional, about 80 percent avail themselves of the nitty-gritty business meetings. They're real contributors, too.

My almost two-hour presentation to this high-spirited group consisted of my wandering through the audience with a wireless microphone in order to stimulate audience participation. I got to talking about warmth at one point, and wanted to know from my listeners what role it played in the life of an accomplished executive.

Warmth is not a common word in describing executive effectiveness, so the response to my question was not immediate. But in a moment or two, one of the spouses raised her hand and offered that warmth has an inspiring side. "It expresses confidence in people," she said, and "it invites them to generate new ideas and actions."

This woman knows that the answer to the question should be "sometimes/seldom."

Confidence in People

Sometime in the last decade, ideas about management set forth thirty to forty years ago by such thinkers as Douglas MacGregor at MIT and Rensis Likert at the University of Michigan took hold. They're not a fad, therefore, because they've been building all this time. Their ideas, all having to do with the trustworthiness of people at work and the fact that people have a stake in and are desirous of doing quality work *together*, are now a prevailing force on the job.

Marty Tretheway, vice president of human resources at Navistar, put it simply and best in a workshop I conducted at that company earlier this week: "This team thing is really catching on!" People want to belong, pull together, and be valued for quality efforts.

Undeniably, we can get burned. Some few people will almost always violate trust, and there's nothing I can say about that. Moreover, all of us know what it means to let others down now and then and not carry our weight. But most consistent failure among people at work is due to a bad *system* at play somehow, and it's clear that as a nation we're cleaning up our act. People care more about their work and about other people. Warmth is in and here to stay.

New Ideas and Actions

The woman in Phoenix said that warmth has an inspiring side. I take that to mean that people are moved to "generate new ideas and actions," as she put it, because trust has been placed in their ability to handle responsibility.

The age of successful tyrants in business is dead or dying. But tyrants do still exist, sadly enough—some still in their forties or even younger. Any managers who still hope to come to true power by controlling, intimidating, and upbraiding subordinates are going to find themselves barking orders up the wrong tree. It is the managers who convey warmth and trust, who know how to elicit ideas instead of squelching them, who will be leaders fit for today's and tomorrow's business climate.

TAKE ACTION

1. Don't be a tyrant. There's no room for one. If you are one, or have a tendency to be one, get new exposures; wake up. See how people are, not how you've beclouded them. It's not too late!

2. Be warm. This doesn't mean change your personality. It means, rather, to trust people with initiative. Let them know you expect it and appreciate it.

99

PROJECTING BIG-PLAY POISE

Q: **Do you feel harried in carrying out your job responsibilities?**

A: Usually/Often _____
Sometimes/Seldom _____

ONE OF THE most recognized, enjoyed, and respected personalities of our day is John Madden. As most readers know, he's a color commentator for CBS pro football telecasts. Almost always, he's paired up with veteran play-by-play announcer Pat Summerall.

We also see Madden—this excitable mountain of a man—doing Lite beer commercials, plumping for Ramada Inns and Ace Hardware Stores, and espousing the virtues of other products and services as well. Moreover, he's the author of two best-selling books.

But what we like most about this spontaneous, unpretentious, enthusiastic, outrageous, hilarious Super Bowl–winning coach turned broadcaster is his joyful competence in converting his formidable knowledge about all facets of the game into a comprehensible whole for a mostly unknowing mass of viewers.

The analogy between sports and business has probably been overspent, but let me keep that abuse going a bit longer. One Sunday afternoon, I heard Madden say that the best quarterbacks "look long before they throw short."

I paid closer attention to quarterbacks such as Joe Montana and Phil Simms from then on and noted their poise: cool under pressure, stepping into the pocket (so the expression goes) in order to ignore the chaos around them, avoid mayhem, and find their receiver. During one Monday night football game, I watched John Elway do this repeatedly, picking apart the vaunted defense of my beloved Chicago Bears.

Looking Long

When a Joe Montana first looks long, he's getting a "sense of the possible" on the play in action. This is an instant inventory of his resources. No matter what he might want to do, he is constrained to be as effective as he can by adapting to conditions as they are. Does the competition have the long receiver covered? Was the tight end taken out of the play from the beginning?

He may have to dump off a short pass to a halfback, or run

for a hole he sees to get a couple of yards, or "eat the ball" and lose a few yards because everything's shut down. But the point is, if he doesn't look long, doesn't size up the whole field, he doesn't gain a sense of the possible.

Stepping Into the Pocket

When Neil Lomax takes the snap, looks long, and sees the possibility for the big play—the long gain, perhaps the touchdown itself—before he can do his job, he has to step into the pocket. This is frightfully hard to do when you see a Richard Dent or Lawrence Taylor coming for you. Yet the pocket is football's eye of the storm. In the pocket is serenity, a gathering of inner resources, an oasis of intense concentration. This is the quarterback's white moment, timeless to him, one to three seconds for everyone watching.

Executives need to step into the pocket, too. If you're going to make the big play, you first must gain a sense of the possible. Then, despite the pressure, threats, risks, and demands of your job, it is imperative that you master the discipline of concentrating on what you need to do rather than listening for footsteps.

The answer to the question should be "sometimes/seldom."

TAKE ACTION

1. Develop your poise by stepping into the pocket. Fortunately, you will have more than a few seconds.
2. At the end of each workday, think about tomorrow. Don't think about the chores you have to do; think about what you're going to *accomplish*.

100

FINDING
THE KITCHEN

Q: Whether long-range or strate-
gic planning is taken seriously
in your company, do *you* give
thought to what it will be
doing twenty-five years from
now?

A: Usually/Often _____
Sometimes/Seldom _____

H ERE'S A NOTION I'd like you to think about with me during the next few minutes: *The future causes the present.*

When my wife and I bought our condominium sixteen years ago, we signed a thirty-year mortgage. The salesman told us at the time, "Things change. People move a lot. Mortgages can be taken out for as long as thirty years, but they average only eight. At that point, they're terminated with the sale of the property."

CEO's usually serve less than a decade. Yet their companies will be affected for years, perhaps for their entire existence, by the future the CEO's choose for them during this relatively short tenure. Certainly today's effort by your CEO, whether or not he likes it, is in many ways directed by a legacy (future) left by previous managements.

An author writing a play may well begin her work with a clear idea of how it is going to end. She writes each day with the knowledge of that end in mind, yet not knowing the content of each day's work until she sits at her desk and it unfolds.

History Consists of Former Futures

When my wife and I signed our mortgage papers for the balance owed on our condominium, our history of payments over the past sixteen years was determined by an agreement that won't be concluded until fourteen years from now.

Jack Akers is the gifted CEO of IBM. He has big ideas stretching well into the next century because he is a big thinker; he couldn't hold *that* job if he weren't. Yet we're all quick to say that a great company like IBM is shaped by its past, and in saying this we're absolutely correct.

But the point I want to make is that the history Akers is expected to build on is a history of *futures* chosen by the Thomas Watsons (Sr. and Jr.), Vincent Learson, Frank Cary, and John Opel.

Philip Roth described the writing of his novel *The Counterlife* in the February 2, 1987, issue of *U.S. News & World Report*:

You're sort of like a busboy in a restaurant, loaded up with dirty dishes—and blindfolded. The guy says 'Find the kitchen.' Well, you may or may not have an accident on the way. If you get to the kitchen and get to the dishwasher, it's an enormous feat.

Reaching the future you've chosen is a feat of comparable difficulty.

Futures Chosen for Us, Futures We Now Choose

It's clear, then, that part of *today's* work in our organizations is to respond to futures chosen (wittingly or unwittingly) by people of the past, and another part is to respond to a future we ourselves choose (also wittingly or unwittingly). This is why the answer to the question should be "usually/often."

Your company's challenge is to find the kitchen, only your lead time is longer than Roth's in writing a single novel. In fact, that kitchen you're looking for is twenty-five years out. A task without a date for completion is not a task, and a job without an appropriate goal is not a job. If your CEO's future does not envision such a twenty-five-year goal, that CEO has created a present that should tell you to travel light and keep your bags packed.

TAKE ACTION

1. Think hard. Know as best you can where your company is headed. As you may remember, in Chapter 97 I wrote that this is what vision is really all about.
2. Ask yourself whether your CEO's a witting chooser or unwitting loser. Lay your plans accordingly. After all, your present performance is dependent on the future *you* choose. Make it a good one!

Your Achiever's Profile

To determine your *achiever's profile*, check your earlier answers against the correct ones listed below. Circle each answer here that corresponds with yours. Then count all your circled answers, and mark your total achiever's profile in the blank provided.

1. U/O	6. S/S	11. U/O	16. S/S	21. U/O
2. U/O	7. S/S	12. S/S	17. S/S	22. S/S
3. S/S	8. U/O	13. U/O	18. U/O	23. U/O
4. S/S	9. U/O	14. S/S	19. U/O	24. S/S
5. U/O	10. S/S	15. U/O	20. S/S	25. S/S
26. S/S	31. U/O	36. U/O	41. S/S	46. S/S
27. S/S	32. U/O	37. U/O	42. S/S	47. U/O
28. S/S	33. U/O	38. U/O	43. S/S	48. U/O
29. U/O	34. S/S	39. S/S	44. U/O	49. S/S
30. S/S	35. S/S	40. S/S	45. U/O	50. U/O
51. U/O	56. S/S	61. U/O	66. U/O	71. S/S
52. S/S	57. U/O	62. U/O	67. S/S	72. U/O
53. S/S	58. U/O	63. S/S	68. U/O	73. S/S
54. U/O	59. U/O	64. S/S	69. S/S	74. S/S
55. U/O	60. S/S	65. U/O	70. S/S	75. S/S
76. U/O	81. S/S	86. S/S	91. U/O	96. S/S
77. U/O	82. U/O	87. U/O	92. S/S	97. U/O
78. S/S	83. U/O	88. S/S	93. S/S	98. S/S
79. S/S	84. U/O	89. U/O	94. U/O	99. S/S
80. U/O	85. U/O	90. S/S	95. U/O	100. U/O

Your Achiever's Profile ————

Superior	92–100
Good	84–91
Satisfactory	68–83
Fair	56–67
Poor	0–55

Index